PRAISE
POWER

The Key

to Happiness in Life

Praise Power - The Key to Happiness in Life
by Dr. Shaun Marler

Published by:
World Harvest Ministries, PO Box 90, Bald Hills, Qld, 4036, Australia
www.bnm.org.au

In partnership with
Spongecake Publishing, PO Box 813, Springwood, Qld, 4127 Australia
www.spongecakepublishing.com

This book or parts thereof may not be reproduced in any form, stored in a retrieval system, or transmitted in any form, by any means - electronic, mechanical, photocopy, recording or otherwise - without prior written permission of the author or publisher, except as provided by Australian copyright law.

All scriptural references taken from the King James Bible unless otherwise stated.

Copyright © Shaun Marler 2019

January 2019

ISBN: 978-0-9871325-1-2

THIS BOOK IS DEDICATED TO
THE EXTENSION OF THE KINGDOM OF GOD.

It is the author's prayer that as you read this teaching, you will allow the Holy Spirit to birth the revelation of the Word of God into your spirit. The Bible declares, "You shall know the truth, and the truth shall make you free".

This powerful revelation of God's Word will bring you the victory.

God's will for your life is abundant love, joy, and peace. May this be yours always.

In Jesus' Name

Pastor Shaun

Foreword

By Dr. Reg Klimionok

During the years that I have known Dr Shaun Marler, I have appreciated his wealth of knowledge and love for God. It was inevitable that our families would become firm friends.

Through time we have had many discussions about our favourite topic (Jesus of course!) and shared our experiences in God. Shaun has explored the realms of the supernatural, and out of his practical Christian living, has written many valuable manuals. The Power of Praise is a gem, and certainly one of his most important books to date.

Inspiring and spiritual, Shaun shows us how to overcome our personal struggles and setbacks and experience God's true blessings for our lives. The Power of Praise is a powerful tool to help you enter a lifestyle that will realise your future in the Kingdom of God.

Dr. Reg Klimionok

Author of "Overcoming the Giants in Your Land"
and "God sent His Angel"

Acknowledgements

I would like to acknowledge the great teachings of Don Gossett and Drummond Thom, dear friends and true fathers in the faith. Their teachings on the subject of Praise have helped me on a personal level, and have blessed my ministry tremendously. Both of them have inspired me to write this book in the hope of blessing others.

Thank You

To everyone who has helped me prepare this book, I extend my gratitude and special thanks: Taryn Marler, Marita Verdouw, Tosh Sturgess, Sarah Freeman and Elmaire Richards for helping me bring this book to completion, Greg Bidell for encouraging me to publish a book, and also to my wonderful wife Kerrie, for her support and constant prayers for this ministry and many contributions to this work.

Contents

Introduction		13
Praise Report 1:	The Wandering Hubcap	14
Chapter One	BEATING THE BLUES	19
Chapter Two	STRESS MANAGEMENT THROUGH THE WORD	23
Chapter Three	PRAYER AND PRAISE	37
Chapter Four	THE FRUIT OF PRAISE	45
Praise Report 2:	The White Leather Jacket	57
Chapter Five	PRAISE AND THOUGHTS	61
Chapter Six	HEBREW MEANING OF PRAISE	67
Chapter Seven	PRAISE IS WORSHIP	73
Praise Report 3:	Epilepsy Healed Through Praise	79
Chapter Eight	PSALM 107	85
Chapter Nine	BENEFITS OF PRAISE	91
Praise Report 4:	The Miracle Weather	97
Chapter Ten	SPIRITUAL WARFARE	101
Chapter Eleven	PRAISE IN WARFARE	107
Chapter Twelve	PRAYING THE SCRIPTURES	113
Praise Report 5:	Praise Brings Favour	123
Chapter Thirteen	PRAISE WALK	125
Praise Report 6:	Kingdom Finance Through Praise	129
Chapter Fourteen	ONE HUNDRED PRAISE SCRIPTURES	133

Praise

Psalm 47: 1-9

Oh, clap your hands, all you peoples!
Shout to God with the voice of triumph!
For the LORD Most High is awesome;
He is a great King over all the earth.
He will subdue the peoples under us,
And the nations under our feet.
He will choose our inheritance for us,
The excellence of Jacob whom He loves. Selah

God has gone up with a shout,
The LORD with the sound of a trumpet.
Sing praises to God, sing praises!
Sing praises to our King, sing praises!
For God is the King of all the earth;
Sing praises with understanding.

God reigns over the nations;
God sits on His holy throne.
The princes of the people have gathered together,
The people of the God of Abraham.
For the shields of the earth belong to God;
He is greatly exalted.

Praise Power

Introduction

This Praise Book is designed to help you journey successfully through life.

God has declared you to be an Overcomer. You were born to win.

You have been designed for accomplishment, engineered for success and endowed with the seeds of greatness. Water those seeds and follow your God-given dream. Live the victorious praise life. Dare to believe the Word of God. Believe in the plan God has for your life.

To gain the most out of this book, do the easy exercises and learn the memory verses. Fill in the answers AND QUOTE OUT LOUD THE WORD OF GOD!

Remember Proverbs 18:21, "Death and life are in the power of your tongue."

Praise Report 1

Testimony of the Wandering Hubcap

In my younger days, I drove a bright green sporty Mazda 929. One day I noticed one of the hubcaps was missing. Now a hubcap cost quite a large sum of money in those days and this particular one was part of a limited edition. Just out of Bible College, recently married with a young baby and serving in a new ministry, my spending habits had definitely been put on hold, so to speak.

Realising that it was beyond my means to purchase a new hubcap, I immediately thanked God that He would bring this hubcap back to me. I prayed "Lord there's nothing concealed that won't be revealed." Even though I had no idea where it could be, I prayed that the angels would take me to my hubcap. Mark 11:24 states: "Therefore I say unto you, what things soever ye desire, when ye pray, believe that ye receive them, and ye shall have them." I prayed this over and over and confessed "Thank you Jesus, thank you for bringing my hubcap back to me. Thank you Father that I have my hubcap back. Father, I have prayed and believed." I used the Praising Principle again and again.

A couple of days passed, and then as I was driving home one day a voice told me to stop and pull over. I did just that. Looking across the field, I spotted my hubcap, lying upside down in the long grass on the other side of the gully. It was only by pulling to the side that I was able to see it, as it was not visible from the road. My heart sang with joy as I picked it up and promptly put it back on, praising God for answering my prayer.

Some months later someone said "Oh, I see you've lost your hubcap." Can you believe it? It was the same hubcap again! I had told everyone about my Praising Principle, and now it seemed as though the devil had stolen it to ruin my testimony. That's what I figured. So I prayed Mark 11:24 again and confessed it. I was immediately attacked with "Like it's going to work again!" However, I stood firm with a "Thank you Father I have my hubcap again. Thank you Jesus for bringing the hubcap back!" practising the Praising Principle. When doubts started to infiltrate my mind, I fought them immediately. I concentrated on 2 Corinthians 10:4-5, which says: "For the weapons of our warfare are not carnal, but mighty through God to the pulling down of strongholds; casting down imaginations, and every high thing that exalteth itself against the knowledge of God, and bringing into captivity every thought to the obedience of Christ."

The devil was trying to get me to doubt whether I would ever see it again. I continued to praise God, thanking Him that His Word works, and I pictured the hubcap in my mind. After a time I went to my brother's house. He said, "By the way, I thought I saw your hubcap sitting on the fence up the road." It was! It had rolled from the road and travelled a considerable distance into a farmer's paddock. The area had been covered with thick, long grass, hiding the silver hubcap. God must have talked to the owner of the paddock about cutting the grass, picking up the hubcap, and putting it on the fence.
Sometimes we think God is not answering our prayers, but it's

just that the circumstances have to line up with His will. He had answered my prayer then and there when I prayed it, but there is a seed time and a harvest time. In the book of Daniel Chapter 10, the angel Gabriel explains a situation to Daniel, how God heard his prayer and dispatched the answer the day he prayed. He goes on to explain that there were spiritual forces from Satan that tried to block the answer. As we keep on praising God and thanking Him, the angels are able to break through the blockages and bring our answers. So I drove down the road, picked up the wandering hubcap and banged it back on the car. By this stage I must admit, I felt like gluing it on, but even then I had a greater testimony of how God had brought back my hubcap.

Talk about my faith being tried! Sometime later on, as I got out of my car, I noticed with astonishment that the hubcap was gone again! Straightaway the devil said to me: "You are not getting it back this time!" Annoyance and doubt flooded through my mind, but I resisted and stood firm on the Praising Principle. Always act rather than react. With every principle in life, we can do one of two things: stay positive or get caught up with negative emotions. If we can learn to act (by applying the Word of God), we can turn a bad circumstance into a good testimony.

Once again I prayed, thanking God and praising God, and calling the hubcap back to my car. Everywhere I drove I would have a little prayer session that the hubcap was already back on. I banished negative thoughts with continual praise. I was determined not to buy another one because I wanted to see God's Word work again. Now three months had passed and still no sign of the hubcap. Then, one day my mother-in-law asked about the hubcap, teasing me with "I thought you said your faith worked? You still don't have your hubcap!" This really annoyed me. I told her that it

PRAISE REPORT 1

would come back and that I had praised God for it. It wasn't lost and the angels knew exactly where it was.

That night I had a bigger praise session than ever before. I thanked God that I was not moved by what I saw, but what I believed. I said, "No way will I buy another one." I praised Him and thanked Him that His Word works. I believed that I had that hubcap. There's a day that God's answer will manifest – so trust Him totally.

I subsequently booked my car in for a service at the local garage. Another man did the same, and as he parked his car beside mine, he noticed that my car's hubcap was missing. He told the serviceman that he found a hubcap similar to those on my car some three months ago in his garden on his front lawn. He subsequently hung it in his garage. This considerate bloke then gave the manager of the garage his address and asked him to tell me to come to his house and pick up my hubcap. Since it was a very distinctive hubcap, he figured it would be very expensive to replace, so he kept it.

Later that afternoon, when I picked up my car, my mechanic told me his other client had my hubcap hanging in his garage and said that I could go and pick it up. After giving me the address, I drove to the man's house and sure enough, down the back of his house, in his garage, was my hubcap. I just praised God for His awesome greatness and thanked Him for His angelic assistants He had sent to assist me in life. I thought about the magnitude of this miracle: that God so arranged it and ordained it through my prayer and praise and trust in Him, that He sent the very man who had my hubcap in his garage to the same mechanic on the same day at the same time in the correct parking space to observe my missing hubcap and realise he was the one with it. The miracle of all this is that God answered my prayer the minute I prayed. God taught me through this incident the awesome power of praise, and to always continue praising especially when the odds are against you.

Well I'm happy to say that that was the last time I lost the wandering hubcap. Shortly afterwards I sold the car!

Chapter 1

Beating the Blues

We read in the book of Deuteronomy 28:47-48 that the price for not serving God with joyfulness and gladness of heart for the abundance of good things that He has done for us, results in us serving our enemies. There are many forces that try to enslave us in life through circumstances and situations we experience. Our attitude or reaction to these life experiences shapes our future. This affects not only us but also those around us and those with whom we come in contact. God does not want you to serve your enemies, but to enjoy His fullness for your life that your joy may be full. He has given us many weapons with which we can win in life. One of these is Praise Power, a liberating force that will flow through you to lift you out of life's valleys and cause you to experience life's joys and triumphs.

Praise is one of the best cures I know for depression. We can never praise Jesus too much. Praise, like sunlight, helps all things grow. Natural life cannot be without sunlight, our Christian life will never be what God has designed it to be without praise.

Depression is one of modern man's biggest problems, affecting large numbers of people from all walks of life. Many other illnesses find their roots in depression. People even take their own lives because of this serious condition. Many hundreds of thousands of dollars are spent on medication to relieve the symptoms of this disease.

If you find yourself wearing a spirit of heaviness or depression, put on the garment of praise. Don't quit, don't give up on life, don't throw the towel in! God loves you, and through praise, He will bring you through whatever difficult situation you are facing right now. Failure is an event, not a person. No matter how grey it looks, the Son is still shining above the clouds of doom, and Praise is your key to the door of the prison you may find yourself in right now. If you can breathe, you can praise.

Praise is the soil in which joy thrives. Let everything that has breath, praise the Lord. God wants you well and whole, full of His love and joy, so that your life can be a testimony to His goodness.

In Psalm 89:15 the Word says "Blessed is the people that know the joyful sound: They shall walk, oh Lord, in the light of Your countenance". We are told in the book of Ephesians 6:10-13, "... be strong in the Lord, and in the power of his might. Put on the whole armour of God, that ye may be able to stand against the wiles of the devil (military strategies of the devil). For we wrestle not against flesh and blood, but against principalities, against powers, against the rulers of the darkness of this world, against spiritual wickedness in high places. Wherefore take unto you the whole armour of God, that ye may be able to withstand in the evil day, (against any of Satan's attacks he sends our way at any given time) and having done all, to stand."

Our God will never leave us or forsake us to the mercy of our enemies. But we can see that we have a part to play in our own victory. Jesus has conquered the powers of darkness on our behalf. Through Him, you are more than a conqueror. However, we must do our part by reinforcing this victory through the mighty weapons that God has placed at our disposal. As we praise our God, we reinforce the victory of Calvary in our lives and circumstances.

Remember 1 Corinthians 15:57 -"But thanks be to God, which giveth us the victory through our Lord Jesus Christ."

As you learn to praise the Lord, you become a doer of the Word and not merely a hearer. The promises of God are activated in our life by faith. God cannot bless ignorance; He tells us to get wisdom and to get understanding. We must learn and understand how to use the Power of Praise to cause His victories to manifest in our lives. Blessed are the people that know the joyful sound for they shall walk in the light of God's revelation, knowledge and divine favour. Praise is a joyful sound to God's ear and praise is a joyful sound to the believer who understands spiritual warfare. God's power, presence and anointing are released as we fill our hearts and mouths with words of praise, releasing with our tongue God's mighty power and faith through His Word.

"To wrestle" in the original Greek means to 'sing' or 'vibrate' and describes a conflict between the Kingdom of Darkness and the Kingdom of Light. As we sing we are in fact fighting the good fight of faith, a fight that has already been fought and won for us by Jesus. This victory now only needs to be established in our lives and circumstances. Psalm 47: 6-8 commands us to, "Sing praises to God, sing praises: sing praises unto our King, sing praises. For God is the King of all the earth: sing ye praises with understanding. God reigneth over the heathen: God sitteth upon the throne of his holiness."

God blesses obedience and our applied knowledge or understanding of His Word. I have written this book for you to study so you can increase your knowledge and understanding of the great Power of Praise. The Lord says, "my people perish for a lack of knowledge." (Hosea 4:6). God blesses intelligence. I challenge you to enthrone God in your life through your praise and worship and allow Him through His Word to reign and rule over every circumstance and event you will ever face. As you follow the leading of His Spirit, walk forward, fulfilling your divine destiny and the great purposes that our wonderful Lord has in store for you.

Better is the end of a thing than its beginning. Your best is yet to come, as you live your life in praise and service to the King.

Nehemiah 8:10 says "Then he said unto them, "Go your way, eat the fat, and drink the sweet, and send portions unto them for whom nothing is prepared: for this day is holy unto our LORD: neither be ye sorry; for the joy of the LORD is your strength."

Proverbs 17:22 tells us that "A merry heart doeth good like a medicine: but a broken spirit drieth the bones."

James 5:13: reminds us: "Is any merry? Let him sing Psalms."

Chapter 2

Stress Management Through The Word

ॐ ॐ

John 14.1 says "Let not your heart be troubled" - these are the words of Jesus to a stressed out world. This Scripture not only contains a command but also a promise from God that He provides an alternative to burnout.

Peace in a troubled world. Strong minded among multitudes of worried minds. Stability in the midst of uncertainty. These are promises to us from God.

Everyone who desires to be all they can be in this world encounters stress. Either we deal with stress or it will deal with us.

In the parable of the sower, Jesus showed us that stress comes immediately when one seeks to progress in life: "...the Word is sown, but when they have heard, Satan cometh immediately and taketh away the word that was sown in their hearts. ...When affliction or persecution ariseth for the word's sake, immediately they are offended." Mark 4:15,17.

The source of pressure is from the world of darkness and its goal is to rob us of the Word of God before it can bear fruit in our lives. If we do not learn the Scriptural way to deal with pressure, we will go from crisis to crisis wasting precious energy. Everyone reacts to pressure, but reacting the Biblical way is the way of victory. You have a choice when you get stressed out - you can let it control you or you can take control of it. Take charge. Becoming a take charge person is not genetic, it is behavioural. It can be learned.

Jesus' disciples were continually amazed at the way He took charge of every circumstance. He never seemed to be in a hurry. There was a calm about Him at all times. It was common for people to say, "What manner of man is this?" Human nature immediately excuses itself by thinking - "He's the Son of God!" Look at this: "But as many as received Him to them gave He power to become Sons of God." John 1:12.

I have two questions for you: Have you received Jesus as your Lord? If so, have you developed the "power to become" all that is a son of God?

1.   SECURE

The starting point of stress management is being secure in who you are. When you don't know who you are, anyone can tell you who they think you are and that's not necessarily who you want to be. Throughout God's Word there are positive affirmations about who you are and what is yours.

2 Corinthians 5:17-21 unveils several wonderful things. First, we are born again, new creations in Christ. He is now our identity and we are complete in Him. Whatever was in our past, it has been

completely wiped out. There is no record of sin or failure against us anymore. God has forgiven us - now we must forgive ourselves.

He has made us righteous in Him, redeemed us from the curse so that all the blessings of His new covenant would be ours, and has given us all things that pertain to life and godliness. As we study God's Word, we discover our identity in our relationship in Christ.

2. ATTITUDE

Someone once said, "Attitude is a small drop that makes a big difference."

A right attitude is more important than ability, circumstances, or social background. Your attitude can cause you to rise above the worst obstacles. It's up to you. You can be a cranky, complaining person or choose to be positive, kind and gracious, a person who continually displays an attitude of gratitude by praising God for what He has done in redeeming us.

You can produce your own atmosphere. The Word says in Proverbs 4:23 to "Keep thy (watch over) heart with all diligence; for out of it are the issues of life." The real issues of life are within you. Settle it forever. From now on a Christ-like attitude will be the order of the day.

3. WORDS ARE CREATIVE

"Death and life are in the power of the tongue." Proverbs 18:21.

Watch what you say. Your words dominate your life whether you realise it or not. Speak faith-filled words. Study the Word of God and find out what the Word promises you and what the Word says about you. Then speak it. Build it into your spirit man. Make yourself strong.

The woman with the issue of blood suffered many things at the hands of many physicians but was not better. She spent all that she had. Then she heard about Jesus.

The Bible tells us that she kept saying, "If I may touch but His clothes, I shall be whole." Mark 5:28. She pressed through the crowds and was made whole. Her confession (positive affirmation of God's Word) motivated her and created the thing she desired.

4. THE IMAGE IN YOUR MIND

In a crisis situation all problems become distorted and magnified. The devil is called the accuser of the brethren. The forces of darkness use threats to paralyse us from moving forward. A threat perceived is usually many times worse than the actual circumstances you are facing.

Images rule us. The woman with the issue of blood had a "grow worse" image. Hope arose through her confession and she replaced it with a "get well" image.

2 Corinthians 10 tells us "to pull down imaginations and every thought that exalts itself above the knowledge of God". Words are image builders. God sent His Word to build an image of victory and success. Pull down the wrong image. Get everything

in the right perspective. Get it in line with the viewpoint from the finished work of Christ.

5. CONSISTENCE & PERSISTENCE

There is a saying that constant dripping wears away the stone. This is a true saying and a powerful life principle can be learned from this. Have you ever been to the river and picked up a rock out of the water? You find that the constant flow of water over this rock has done exactly that, worn away the stone. The tiny, minute, microscopic particles carried along in the constant stream have worn away the properties of that mighty stone. The rough jaggered rock had yielded in time to the softer substance of water.

In our consistence and persistence of praising and of declaring God's Word lies the power. The book of Luke 11 gives an excellent illustration. A friend asks for help at midnight. The man from whom the help was sought would not get out of bed to give him what he needed, due to the lateness of the hour. However, because of this man's insistence and persistence, he eventually arises and gives him all that he required. The Bible tells us in the book of Proverbs 24:10 "that if we faint in the day of adversity our strength is small". We need to draw a line in the sand, rise up and deal with life and its pressures, because Philippians 4:13 promises "we can {you can} do all things through Christ who strengthens us."

A great man once said "My great concern is not whether you have failed but whether you are content with failure." This man was qualified to make this statement for he was a living example of his own convictions.

Let me outline for you a brief summary of some of the events of his life:

Failed in business in 1831

Defeated for legislature in 1832

Second failure in business in 1833

Suffered nervous breakdown in 1836

Defeated for speaker in 1838

Defeated for elector in 1840

Defeated for Congress in 1843

Defeated for Congress in 1848

Defeated for Senate in 1855

Defeated for Vice President in 1856

Defeated for Senate in 1858

ELECTED PRESIDENT OF U.S.A. in 1860

ABRAHAM LINCOLN

Abraham Lincoln was also quoted as saying: "Always bear in mind your own resolution to succeed is more important than any other one thing."

Henry Ford said "Failure is but the opportunity to begin again more intelligently."

6. GO ON THE ATTACK

It's time to draw a line in the sand and say "NO MORE MR. DEVIL, I AM THE SEED OF ABRAHAM!" Galatians 3:29 tells us: "If you be Christ's, then you are Abraham's seed and heirs according to the promise of God."

Jesus said "According to your faith be it unto you." This does not sound like a haphazard style of living. Faith is not "fate". Fate says what will be will be. Faith says, God said it, I believe and that settles it. Faith takes hold of what God has promised and presses into it.

General Patton said "To defend, you must attack." Rise up, take charge of your life and manage your pressure.

"Know your enemy and know yourself and you will not be in peril in a thousand battles" The Art of War - Sun Tsu.

It is time to praise the Lord. You need to take the offensive position by taking the fight to the heart of the enemy's camp. You do this through words of praise as you declare your confidence in God, speaking forth His Word boldly in expressions of adoration of the greatness of His power and person.

7. ASSOCIATIONS

I read an article from Brisbane's Courier Mail (Wednesday September 5th, 2001, pg. 31), written by Michael D. Yapko. Michael is a clinical psychologist and depression expert from the United States. The article was titled, '*Depression May Depend on Who You Know.*' In this article, Michael says that the 'blues' are contagious, and a single pill isn't the answer.

Can you catch a depressed mood the same way you catch a cold? Not exactly, but similar. Can other people really be a source of the rising rate of depression in Australia? The scientific evidence suggests the answer is, yes.

Our social lives play a huge role in how we think and feel. After all, none of us are immune to the influence of others, for better or worse. How we react to others, and vice versa, even has a measurable biological impact on brain chemistry, as the newest brain research shows us. The evidence is rapidly mounting that depression is much more then just an individual's "bad chemistry". Thinking of depression as a brain disease is a perspective that is proving to be too one dimensional.

This rising rate of depression is not unique to Australians, lending further support to the growing recognition of depression being spread across borders through social means. Through the studies of cultures, families, and the social lives of depressed people, we have learned a great deal about the social transmission of depression. Negative people can bring us down, and good relationships involving an enduring commitment can bring us up.

We have also learned how children model their parents in

unexpected ways that increase their vulnerability to depression. Thus in a purely social sense, depression is contagious.

The World Health Organisation (WHO) recently declared depression the fourth greatest cause of human suffering and disability in the world behind heart disease, cancer, and traffic accidents. Even more troubling, the WHO predicts that by the year 2020 depression will have risen to become the second greatest cause of human disability and suffering.

By focusing on biology alone, as we have done when we talk about chemical imbalances in the brain or calling depression a "disease", the social dimension has been all but ignored. This allows the social conditions that cause and exacerbate depression in many people's lives to go unaddressed. Michael D. Yapko says, "Drugs alone cannot address the social factors that underlie depression, a likely reason that drug treatment alone (without additional skill-building treatments) has the highest rate of relapse of any form of intervention.

Just as there will never be a pill that can cure other largely social issues such as poverty or racism, there will never be a pill that will cure the depression that is associated with challenging life conditions. This is not to say biology doesn't matter. It clearly does. But to focus on biology to the exclusion of the life circumstances, especially the social ones, that lead people into depression is missing a vital target of intervention."

Too often, well-intentioned doctors write a prescription for an anti-depressant medication but go no further in their treatment. The evidence is growing that this practice is, to put it mildly, less than ideal.

The new understandings about the prominence of social forces in depression require us to change some of what we do as we try to educate people about depression.

The familiar phrasing that suggests "depression is a serious medical illness requiring medication" is an educational approach that simply doesn't work very well. Most of the people who are depressed don't seek help. For some, it's because they simply don't think of themselves as "diseased".

In fact, most people who suffer depression still manage to function despite their condition. They show up for work, they participate in family events, but they are struggling to get through each day. They are what many clinicians refer to as the "walking wounded".

We can do better than suggest to people they're diseased and need drug cures. We can do more than continuing to push the one-dimensional biological explanation at people for their depression. We can help them understand that depression is caused by many different contributing factors of which some are indeed biological, while others are rooted in individual psychology (such as your temperament and style of coping with stress) and social psychology (such as the quality of your relationships and your culturally acquired views).

Striving to convince people they're diseased doesn't empower them to actively change their lives in meaningful ways. We can teach better relationship skills, better problem-solving skills and better ways to cope with an increasingly complex world.

These are the skills that have not only been shown to reduce depression, but even to prevent it.

I believe that once we learn to praise God effectively, by declaring His word joyously and boldly back to Him on a daily basis, we will have a powerful skill and weapon to defeat the enemy of depression that tries to attack our lives and bring us down. I remember reading that Kenneth Hagin said in one of his books that the anointing or atmosphere on our lives is affected by our influences, environment and associations. The Word of God brings us warning in Proverbs 22:24-25, "Make no friendship with an angry man; with a furious man you shall not go: Or you will learn his ways, and get a snare to your soul."

From the above article, and from the Word of God, we can learn how our associations affect us. I remember reading once that during the course of our lives we actually influence over 10,000 people, one way or another. We need to learn to be or become a positive influence on our families, workmates and those we rub shoulders with in life. The bible says that a merry heart does us good like a medicine, but a broken spirit dries the bones (Proverbs 17:22).

Through praising God, and keeping His joy in our hearts, we will actually be doing ourselves good. Praise is good medicine and very uplifting if and when we have the blues. We need to not only be a praiser or practice the skill of praise, but we need to form friendships with people who have a happy, healthy outlook on life. This is not always possible in our workplaces or social circles in which we move. I suggest you find a good church that knows how to praise God with good home-fellowships. You can meet people for the purpose of forming new and vital relationships and associations. Here, in these relationships, you can pray for one another and uphold one another's burdens, by having times when you all praise God and speak His promises. This encourages others and you also get lifted up and encouraged. Then as you go to your work environments or other social circles, you will go built up and encouraged so you can be a positive influence and an inspiration to others.

Failure is not a person, but an event that is only temporary and can be overcome by the blood of the lamb and the word of your testimony (Revelation 12:11). God never made a failure when He made you. You are an Overcomer, you have been endowed with the seeds of greatness, designed for accomplishment and engineered for success. You are a somebody, because you were made by God, and He doesn't waste His time to make nobodies. You are unique, one of a kind, and as the bible says, the apple of your Heavenly Father's eye. He loves you so much that He sent His only son, the Lord Jesus Christ to die for you, to give you victory and everlasting life.

We can, to a certain extent control our environment. Maybe not always, in every situation, because we do have to travel around and work in environments over which sometimes we have no control or influence. But, when it comes to our homes, our cars, and sometimes our workstations, we need to bring into these places good, wholesome and positive things. The music we choose to listen to is very important in defeating depression in our lives. We must predominately listen to music and lyrics that build us up and encourage us. There is an abundance of excellent worship and praise music that you will find very edifying and soul-lifting. It also can cause us to want to burst out in spontaneous praise and thanksgiving to God.

Influences can also be very helpful in maintaining a positive attitude of praise. I find it very encouraging to read God's Word regularly, and the life stories of people who have overcome great odds and difficulties to achieve success in their chosen fields of endeavour. As often as I can, I sit down with people who have achieved breakthrough in their life. I find, that by listening to their personal testimonies I am encouraged to press on and praise through every trial and obstacle I face in life. If you can find a mentor, then I encourage you to do so. The Bible says that one can put a thousand to flight, but two, ten thousand. There is nothing like having someone that has walked the path you are walking and can point out pit-falls and road-blocks along the way to help you reach your destination.

Jesus said (in His teachings), be careful what you see and what you hear. We have to be very cautious what we constantly listen to and expose ourself to in life. These things have an influence over us, our thinking and our moods. Our behaviour can be affected very strongly by what has influenced us in the past. So like the Apostle Paul says in Philippians 4, "Whatsoever things are true, whatsoever things are honest, whatsoever things are just, whatsoever things are lovely, whatsoever things are of good report, if there be any virtue, if there be any praise, think on these things, copy His example, learn of Him and the God of peace shall be with you."

Chapter 3

Prayer and Praise

2 Timothy 3:1-2 reveals to us, "This know also, that in the last days perilous times shall come. For men shall be lovers of their own selves, covetous, boasters, proud, blasphemers, disobedient to parents, unthankful, unholy..."

The word here that I want to emphasise is unthankful.

The Bible tells us, one of the conditions of men's hearts in the last days, is that they will be unthankful.

Philippians 4:4-6 reminds us to "Rejoice in the Lord always: and again I say, Rejoice. Let your moderation be known unto all men. The Lord is at hand. Be careful for nothing; but in every thing by prayer and supplication with thanksgiving let your requests be made known unto God."

We are instructed to rejoice in the Lord always, and again to rejoice. That means to do it over and over, over and over, and over again. Keep on rejoicing. The verse goes on to tell us that the Lord is at hand, that we should be careful for nothing, but in everything, by prayer and supplication with thanksgiving, we should let our requests be made known unto God.

To be careful for nothing, means to cast all your cares, worries, and anxieties, upon the Lord. It does not mean to be slack or slothful in your business, personal life or family matters. Rather, it means to put your trust in the Lord, in all circumstances of life, trusting Him for a favourable outcome. Trust that God will look after you, and care for you!

We are always asking God to do things for us – to provide things for us – but we must remember to thank Him for His provision of our every need through Jesus Christ and the cross of Calvary.

Remember the Lord is at hand. One day the Lord spoke very strongly into my spirit and said "Shaun, I am at hand, I never leave you or forsake you, I am right there at your hand, I am here for you."

Until this time I had always taken this verse and used it as a reference to Jesus' second coming. But now God was revealing to me a much more powerful revelation and that is, GOD IS ALWAYS NEAR AT HAND AND READY TO HELP.

He loves you and will never leave or forsake you. The hand of the Lord is not short that, He cannot save, neither is His ear deaf that He cannot hear. He is rich to all those who call upon Him.

I always like to say,

"IF YOU WANT SOMETHING YOU HAVE NEVER HAD, YOU HAVE TO DO SOMETHING YOU HAVE NEVER DONE."

FAITH WORK

James 1:22 tells us "But be doers of the Word (obey the message), and not merely listeners to it, betraying yourselves (into deception by reasoning contrary to the Truth)."

Now write out ten things to rejoice over and be thankful to God (for e.g. your salvation.)

1. _____
2. _____
3. _____
4. _____
5. _____
6. _____
7. _____
8. _____
9. _____
10. _____

Thank God for these ten blessings now.
      List them out to Him.
           Speak them.
                Mean it!

As we learn to call upon Him, out of a heart filled with thanksgiving, His presence and goodness will be manifest in our midst.

Prayer and praise are the thermometers of the Spirit. When prayer is accompanied by praise, we put ourselves in line for the blessings of God to be manifest in our lives. Prayer and praise are the two wings with which we, like eagles, mount up into the heavenlies and fly with our God.

1 Peter 2:9 tells us "But ye are a chosen generation, a royal priesthood, a holy nation, a peculiar people; that ye should shew forth the praises of Him who hath called you out of darkness into His marvelous light".

We see the primary function of the born-again believer is to show forth the praises of God.

God is looking for people after His own heart- like David the Psalmist.

2 Chronicles 16:9 explains, "For the eyes of the Lord run to and fro throughout the whole earth, to shew Himself strong in the behalf of them whose heart is perfect toward Him. ..."

People who will praise Him with thankful hearts.

God tells us in Psalm 50:23 "Whoso offereth praise glorifieth Me: and to him that ordereth his conversation aright will I shew the salvation of God."

Whosoever offers praise, glorifies God! And if that was all it said, that would be enough to go on praising forever! God commands our praise. God is worthy of our praise. God inhabits our praise. God delights and takes pleasure in our praise.

But NO! The scripture does not stop there, it goes on to say: "and to him that orders his conversation aright will I shew the salvation of God."

Salvation is not just the saving of the soul from destruction, but it is also being saved from sickness, poverty, depression and every evil plan the enemy would try to inflict upon us! 1 John 5:18 says, "He that is begotten of God (i.e. Born Again Believer) keepeth himself, and that wicked one toucheth him not."

Here we have a beautiful promise from God. If we offer a sacrifice of praise unto God, we are magnifying God over our lives, over our problems; we are exalting God. As we do this, we are bringing our tongue into gear, or in line with God's Word (by ordering our conversation aright) which, in turn is going to open the way, clear the channel, for the blessings of God to flow.

FAITH WORK

Pray the Word to God.

Then praise the Word to God.

By doing this, we will not only have the ear of God ("For God watches over His Word to perform it." Jer 1:12), but also the ear of the angels which are sent forth by God to minister for the saints.

Hebrews 1:14 explains it this way "Are not the angels all ministering spirits (servants) sent out in the service (of God for the assistance) of those who are to inherit salvation?"

Psalm 103:20 "Bless (affectionately, gratefully praise) the Lord, you His angels, you mighty ones who do His commandments, hearkening to the voice of His Word."

Praise waters the Word which is like a seed, allowing it to spring forth and grow, bringing forth a harvest for us.

1 Peter 1:23 establishes us: "having been born again, not of corruptible seed but incorruptible, through the word of God which lives and abides forever"

AND GOD IS GOING TO MANIFEST HIS PROMISES,
AND SHOW US, DECLARE TO US,
HIS SALVATION.

There is no way that you can ever make God any bigger than He already is, yet the Word says, as we Praise the Lord, we magnify Him. So what does this mean? It means that your Praise to God, makes God and His Word in your life, bigger than the problems you are facing. Praise glorifies God, Who is your salvation, and your answer. Doubt and unbelief only glorifies the problems, and diminishes God's influence in your life.

This teaching on Praise in no way contradicts any teaching we have had on the Word or Prayer!

Philippians 4:6 declares "... in everything by prayer and supplication with thanksgiving ..." Colossians 4:2 reads "Continue in prayer, and watch in the same with thanksgiving".

In actual fact, prayer and praise must never be separated.

Chapter 4

The Fruit of Praise

WHAT DOES IT MEAN TO PRAISE'?

The dictionary meaning of praise is: to laud the glory of God, as in song, glorify, commendation, glorification, to praise someone highly, to commend their worth, express admiration.

'Laud' means to loudly proclaim or declare. Be 'vocal' – using the words of your mouth.

Hebrews 13:15 "By Him therefore let us offer the sacrifice of praise to God continually, that is, the fruit of our lips giving thanks to His name."

As we offer the sacrifice of praise (which under this covenant is the sacrifice that God requires), giving thanks unto His name for what He has done for us, we are offering the fruit of our lips.

John 15:8 tells us "Herein is my Father glorified, that ye bear much fruit; so shall ye be my disciples."

Our Father is glorified as we, His disciples, bear much fruit. The more we praise, the more fruit we bear. Little praise = little fruit. No praise = no fruit. Much Praise = Much Fruit.

Job 6:25 "How forcible are right words! But what doth your arguing reprove?"

Forcible means powerful. Words of praise are right and powerful in the realm of the Spirit.

Ecclesiastes 8:4 explains: " Where the word of a King is, there is power."

As we praise the King of all kings, by using Word of God, we release the greatest power.

Psalm 92:14 "They shall still bring forth fruit in old age: they shall be fat and flourishing"

WHETHER YOUNG OR OLD
WE SHALL BRING FORTH MUCH FRUIT
BY PRAISING HIM.

Psalm 50:23 "Whoso offereth praise glorifieth Me: and to him that ordereth his conversation aright will I shew the salvation of God."

The Father partakes of the fruit of our lips and it pleases Him. We order our conversation according to His word, and He shows us His salvation.

FAITH WORK

James 1:22 "But be ye doers of the word, and not hearers only, deceiving your own selves."

Hebrews 13:15 "By Him therefore let us offer the sacrifice of praise to God continually, that is, the fruit of our lips, giving thanks to His name."

Under this new covenant, God requires a different sacrifice to the old covenant. The sacrifice that God now requires is the sacrifice of

_____

How often should we offer this type of sacrifice?

_____

Go to your dictionary and find the meaning of the word continually. Now write it down below.

_____

_____

Isaiah 57:19 "I create the fruit of the lips; Peace, peace to him that is far off, and to him that is near, saith the Lord; and I will heal him."

God literally creates the fruit of our lips – that is, our praise. Our thanksgiving to Him for all that He is, for all that He has done, and for all that He will do for us, His redeemed people.

Proverbs 12:14 "A man shall be satisfied with good by the fruit of his mouth: and the recompense of a man's hands shall be rendered unto him."

Proverbs 18:20-21 "A man's belly shall be satisfied with the fruit of his mouth; and with the increase of his lips shall he be filled. Death and life are in the power of the tongue: and they that love it shall eat the fruit thereof."

What you say causes increase, either negative or positive increase!!

The Word declares a man's belly shall be satisfied with the fruit of his mouth.

> Remember that our Praise
> Is the fruit of our own lips.

It goes on to say that with the increase of our lips we shall be filled, so that praise, and an increase of praise in our life, will result in more fulfillment, more satisfaction and enjoyment in life.

Remember Verse 21 says "Death and life are in the power of the tongue: and they that love it shall eat the fruit thereof." We are commanded by God in Deuteronomy 30:19 to choose life so that we and our seed may live and enjoy life.

As we choose words of praise, instead of words of doubt and unbelief, we are choosing words of life. God's life-giving words are being spoken by us. We can speak these life-giving praise words into our family, our children and any and all circumstances of life. Remember death and life are in the power of your tongue. Your tongue has power – the power of death and life – so use your tongue very wisely, and speak words of praise.

Choose life and speak it forth. Words are like seeds, the Bible says, so plant the right seeds, the right words, that grow trees of life, health, goodness, and prosperity. We are promised in the book of Proverbs that health and healing is in the tongue of the wise.

Proverbs 15:4 "A wholesome tongue is a tree of life: but perverseness therein is a breach in the spirit".

Proverbs 12:18 "There is that speaketh like the piercings of a sword: but the tongue of the wise is health."

Deuteronomy 30:19 "I call heaven and earth to record this day against you, that I have set before you life and death, blessing and cursing: therefore choose life, that both you and your seed may live."

I challenge you this day to bear abundant lip fruit by practicing the praising principle, and starting to praise God more and more till your praise becomes habitual –
WITH CONSISTENCY LIES THE POWER.

It takes fifty facial muscles to frown, but only sixteen to smile!

If Jesus saved you, He wants to give you:

- A spring in your step.
- A song in your heart.
- A smile on your dial.
- A real zest for living.

Practice Praise Power! God has power to lift your spirit, loose you from your bondages, and give you victory in every circumstance.

The Lord has given us the joy of His Salvation, that we might in return offer to Him, Praises continually.

God Never Does Anything By Chance.

Notice how God finishes the Book of Psalms? Psalm 150:6 "Let every thing that hath breath praise the Lord. Praise ye the Lord."

That's the last verse of the last Psalm: "Let every thing that hath breath praise the Lord. Praise ye the Lord."

The Hebrew name for the Book of Psalms is simply the equivalent to the word 'praises', and is actually a bit more appropriate than 'Psalms', which comes from the Greek!

There is something about the nature of God that demands our praises.

Why? Because God lives in, dwells in, inhabits, our praises. We are told in Psalm 22:3 "But thou art holy, O thou that inhabitest the praises of Israel."

The word "inhabitest" here actually means, to live in, dwell, reside continually, make His abode. God takes up residence in the praise of His people. If you want to bring the presence of God down on the scene, then praise Him. If you want God's intervention in a matter, speak words of praise, for praise brings the presence of God, as He dwells in the praises of His people.

The true spirit of Praise does not drive people away, it attracts them.

Jesus said in John 12:32, "if I be lifted up (and that is what we are doing when we praise Him) then I will draw all men unto Me."

It is the Holy Spirit who draws us unto God. You see, as we praise Him with honest hearts, as we worship Him with all our hearts, then, collectively or corporately, He is manifest in our praise. The glory of God, and the presence of God, are linked to our praising Him.

As we get a manifestation of the presence of God amongst us, lives are touched, people feel good, the anointing of the Spirit of God ministers to people and people are drawn to Christ. People are edified. Unsaved people who don't know God, get saved because they are drawn to this beautiful presence of God. Finally, the vacuum within them can be filled with Jesus Christ.

Let's look at Acts 2:47: "Praising God, and having favour with all the people, and the Lord added to the church daily such as should be saved."

FAITH WORK

QUESTIONS AND ANSWERS FROM TEACHING TO DATE.

1. What will an increase in praise do or result in?

_____

_____

_____

2. What is in the power of your tongue?

_____

_____

_____

3. According to Isaiah 57:19, what does God create?

_____

_____

_____

4. What do we do when we glorify God by praising Him? (Hint – Psalm 50:23)

_____

_____

_____

5. What will be the condition of some peoples' hearts in the last days?

_____

_____

_____

6. How can we avoid this?

_____

_____

_____

7. According to Philippians 4:4, what should we do all the time?

_____

_____

The early Christians were "Praising God and having favour with all the people, and the Lord added to the Church daily, such as should be saved". People desire reality in Christ. They don't want a dead tradition, a worthless formality. People crave reality.

When we praise the Lord, we are not being obnoxious or disorderly. Praises unto the Lord are beautiful, harmonious with heaven, and are pleasing to God.

> You can't get under a manifestation
> of the Glory of God,
> without wanting to Praise Him.

Psalm 147:1 "Praise ye the Lord: for it is good to sing praises unto our God; for it is pleasant; and praise is comely."

The Hebrew meaning of comely is 'beautiful, becometh, suitable' (it becomes the upright to praise God). This means it is appropriate for the upright to praise God.

Psalm 33:1 "Rejoice in the Lord, O ye righteous; for praise is beautiful for the upright."

People in the world get so excited at a wrestling match or a football game. They holler and shout and cheer and scream. They get passionate! How much more should we get inspired about our God?

Man's order is religious worship, ceremonial, ritualistic, or formal:

God's order is dignity, life, and liberty.
There is absolutely nothing undignified about praising the Lord, nor is there anything indecent about praising the Lord!

Let's look at Jesus and his attitude toward praise. If Jesus gets nervous about praise, then we ought to as well; but if he doesn't, then we shouldn't either.

Luke 19:37-40   "And when He was come nigh, even now at the descent of the mount of Olives, the whole multitude of the disciples began to rejoice and praise God with a loud voice for all the mighty works that they had seen; saying, 'Blessed be the King that cometh in the Name of the Lord: peace in heaven, and glory in the highest.' And some of the Pharisees from among the multitude said unto Him, 'Master, rebuke thy disciples.' And He answered, and said unto them, 'I tell you that, if these should hold their peace, the stones would immediately cry out.'"

We see here that Jesus did not get nervous, it was the Pharisees who did. The world doesn't get nervous when we praise the Lord - it's religious folk who get nervous.

Jesus is for Praise! Praise continually takes place in heaven. Revelation 5:11-12 gives us some insight: "And I beheld, and I heard the voice of many angels round about the throne and the beasts and the elders: and the number of them was ten thousand times ten thousand, and thousands of thousands; Saying with a loud voice, Worthy is the Lamb that was slain to receive power, and riches, and wisdom, and strength, and honour, and glory, and blessing."

Joy leaps!, Joy shouts!, Joy has strength! Joy has Power!
Joy rejoices!!

If your heart is full of praise and joy for the God of your salvation, it will be evident in your life.

Praise Report 2

The White Leather Jacket

Many years ago when I first entered the ministry, God taught me a powerful lesson about praise. As God had blessed us with some finances, my wife Kerrie and I went shopping to buy clothes I could minister in. In a shop I came across a striking white leather jacket. I had never seen one before and decided to try it on. Surprisingly, it fitted me perfectly. The white leather jacket looked great, smelt great and felt great. I turned to Kerrie and said, "This would be excellent for me to travel in and also for when I minister."

It was slightly more than I wanted to pay, so I needed to draw additional funds out of the bank. I asked the sales lady to keep the jacket for me and promptly went to look for an automatic teller machine. Upon returning to the shop with the extra money, the saleslady casually informed me that she had sold the jacket! I couldn't believe my ears and obviously wasn't too happy about it. I reminded her that she promised to put it aside for me until I had been to a bank. She said something like "Sorry, it's gone and there is absolutely nothing I can do about it." She offered to ring other stores in the State to find one.

The saleslady commenced ringing around and, to my dismay, was told that there were none left anywhere. I was extremely disappointed in this because, unlike other jackets, the sleeves had fitted my long arms perfectly. We left our phone number, even though the saleslady said it was pointless.

When I went home, I told Kerrie I was so mad that the devil had got to that lady by prompting her to sell it. I told my wife I was going to believe for that jacket. So I prayed and asked the Father for a jacket exactly like that one. Then I commenced praising God. I praised Him profusely: "Thank you God that I have a white leather jacket that fits me perfectly." "Thank you that I have received a white leather jacket that I will be able to use when I travel." And: " I have the white leather jacket now, I am not moved that there's none left. I'm going to thank You and praise You now for it."

I had been very annoyed at the shop assistant, and had to make peace with her in my heart, so I said "Lord, I forgive that saleslady as it is not her fault. It is the devil that caused this mishap just to inconvenience and annoy me. Father, I am going to see Your miraculous ability; You are greater, more powerful than he is. I am going to maintain an attitude of gratitude, and I am going to praise You for Your awesome ability Lord. The things that are impossible for man are possible for You God. I don't / won't believe that there are none left". I thank You for my white leather jacket to preach in." I refused to become discouraged, and for the next couple of days I thanked Him over and over for His provision and for my white leather jacket.

Now you might say, "why get upset about a white leather jacket?" You're right, for I had to deal with those feelings, so I thanked God for His goodness and asked Him to bless the lady who had

PRAISE REPORT 2

broken her word to me, and I made sure that I forgave her and that I kept my attitude right. It is very important to keep a positive, forgiving attitude towards others, for I have discovered that our attitude towards life, circumstances, and others has a great bearing on the future outcome of events. As author of the best-seller *'The Winning Attitude'*, John Maxwell says, "Our attitude determines our altitude". In other words, our attitude determines the extent to which we fail or succeed in life. Success is a journey not a destination, and an attitude of gratitude will keep us going in the right direction.

I wanted to see God's awesome ability at work and see Him turn the situation around. It wasn't about a white leather jacket any more. It was about the devil stealing from me and my feelings of disappointment. I wanted to see my feelings overcome by praise and Satan defeated in this. I also believed God's creative ability could work for me and that the God of the universe would fulfill the desire of my heart. Read the inspiring scripture in Psalm 37:4 "Delight thyself also in the Lord; and He shall give thee the desires of thine heart."

I had learnt that "...death and life are in the power of the tongue." Proverbs 18:21. I decided to ignore the negative report that there was not another white leather jacket in the country and instead concentrated on the creative power of God Almighty. Romans 4:17 teaches: "even God, who... calleth those things which be not as though they were..." Therefore I could say with confidence, "In Jesus' name, I have a white leather jacket that fits me perfectly, Amen." For the next couple of days I practised the Praising Principle and continually thanked God for His goodness towards me.

About three days later the shop assistant phoned me. She informed me that she had been able to contact the manufacturer of the jacket. Incidentally, I hadn't asked her to do that. God had obviously spoken to her heart. She had found out that the manufacturer had just enough white leather left to make one more jacket, and if I still wanted one, I had to give her the go ahead. She would even give me a discount for my inconvenience! I thanked her from the bottom of my heart and gave her the go ahead. Suffice to say, I got many good years of use out of the white leather jacket before I gave it away.

Our God is an awesome God, and His Word works when we work the Word.

Chapter 5

Praise and Thoughts

Let us praise Him, no matter what God asks or expects of us; let us praise Him in every situation of life. Let us praise Him no matter what He appoints or calls us to do. Let us take great joy in Him, reverence Him and respect Him in everything that concerns Him. Let Him be 'God' to us, our exceeding joy (Psalm 34:4).

Do you know what it is to delight yourself in God? Learn to enjoy God, enjoy His love, enjoy His presence. As you enjoy Him, offer Him continued praise. Life is no longer to be sorrowful, even amid sorrow, when you know Him and invite Him through praise to be part of your life. No matter how strained, trying or hopeless your circumstances, no matter how afflicted your life, life is worth the living when you honour God. We just need to taste His life in us and experience the joy of the Lord, which God guarantees will be our strength. Remember 'God' the Lord God, allows you to call Him 'Father'. He is your answer, your deliverance, your 'Daddy' God and He loves you.

Praise is heart enjoyment, heart enlightenment. Praise is life-giving, spirit-lifting and soul-empowering. Praise is ready to pick you up and set you free from whatever enslaves you. God has done so much for me that I must praise Him, or feel as if I had a fire shut up within me: a force that I cannot contain, but must release. Our God is longing for His people to praise Him (Psalm 107).

The Lord has favoured you greatly. Before the earth was, He chose you and entered into a covenant with you. He gave you to His son Jesus and He gave His son Jesus to you. When we accept Him and what He has done for us, when we believe on His name, He breathes His Spirit into us, so we can say 'Abba, Father' or 'my Daddy God' (Romans 8:15). Surely you must praise Him! How can we ever be totally satisfied in life if we do not praise Him? To truly satisfy the deep longing of our heart or spirit we must learn to exalt, honour and praise the Lord our God.

We need to launch out into His sea of Love and express our deepest appreciation to Him for who He is and what He has done for us. Your name is written in the Lamb's book of Life. Through Him you will live forever.

Learn to practise the presence of God. Through praise, even in the midst of trouble, learn to enjoy God. Let God swallow you up in His immense love, let Him wrap His arms of comfort and reassurance around you. As the old Hymn says "What a friend we have in Jesus, all our sins and griefs to bear; what a privilege to carry everything to God in prayer." You will build a nest for your soul in the presence of a loving Jesus. He will swallow you up in the fathomless abyss of His infinite love. God wants to pour out His affection upon you. Just as Leah when Judah (Hebrew meaning of Judah is Praise) was born, let us say, "Now will I praise the Lord!" (Genesis 29:35).

FAITH WORK

Right now let's do an exercise that a good friend of mine taught me to do.

His name is Don Gossett. This is one of his Praising Power Principles.

Raise both hands right now!

Say out loud ten times: PRAISE THE LORD.

Say these words right this very minute. Let's go!
                              S H O U T – BE VOCAL

PRAISE THE LORD
PRAISE THE LORD
PRAISE THE LORD
PRAISE THE LORD
PRAISE THE LORD
PRAISE THE LORD
PRAISE THE LORD
PRAISE THE LORD
PRAISE THE LORD
PRAISE THE LORD

It's time for us to give birth to praise. Let us bring praise forth and release God's joy and goodness on the earth. Let us bring hope to hopeless situations by praising Him.

Could we ever love anyone as we love our God? Yet often we lavish praise on things or someone we love, while we neglect to adore God. When we focus our attention on our God, and we start to unashamedly praise Him with passion and energy, oh what a joy will flood back to our own souls. We need to surrender our reason to His revelation, learn to trust in Him and hope in His Word. That which we cannot understand, we nevertheless believe, and believing, we adore and trust Him! We must learn to submit to Him, we are His servants and He is supremely good. He is our Creator and only has our best interests at heart.

Every believer must discover for himself the power and benefits of praise. I can write about them, you can hear and read the testimonies of others, but only when you start to offer the sacrifice of praise to God continually, will you know the reality of this power and the joy it brings to your own life. Psalms and hymns and spiritual sayings should resound in our homes. It is our duty to praise as much as possible.

The world is full of song. Every sporting event is marked by praise for one's team. Should we, as Christians, be ashamed to praise our King for all He has done for us? You might say, "But I don't have a good voice!" If you can't sing, then speak or make a joyful noise unto God. Everyone can speak of His wonderful works and declare the great things He has done. Death and life are in the power of the tongue. We need to flavor our conversations with the praise of God and fill our mouths with words of life.

It is easy to judge, criticise, pull down and complain. Homes are being destroyed today, because of verbal abuse. Many a person has a damaged personality, because at one time they were a victim of soul-destroying words. But now we have an answer, now we can find healing for our souls or bring healing to another by choosing to praise the Word of God and speaking encouraging, uplifting words to ourselves and others. The Bible says to let your words impart grace and faith to the hearers. It is time to mend our talk and speak lovingly and cheerfully of what God has done for us.

It is time to put an end to murmurings and gossip. If you make a mistake and are momentarily caught up in this kind of attitude, repent and redeem yourself. Ask God to forgive you, and return to praise, gratitude and thanksgiving straight away. Hear the Word of the Lord which says, "Neither murmur you, as some of them also murmured, and were destroyed by the destroyer" (1 Corinthians 10:10). "Satan goes around as a roaring lion... seeking whom he may devour" (1 Peter 5:8). Jesus said "The thief comes to steal, kill and destroy" (John 10:10). Give Satan no place. Don't let him gain an advantage over you through wrong words.

Praise means this: that you and I are appointed to tell forth the goodness of God. Just as the birds wake up before the sun rises and begin singing – and singing with all their might – so we are to become the choristers of God. Praise the Lord evermore, even as they do, with songs and choral symphonies. Day and night, circle His throne rejoicing. This is your holy and privileged office.

These lips of ours must produce fruit. The praise of God is the fruit that can be stored up and presented to the Lord. Fruit is a natural product. It grows without force, the free outcome of the plant. So let praise grow out of your lips at its own accord. Let it be as natural to you, as regenerated men and women, to praise God as it seems natural to profane men to blaspheme His sacred name.

Stand up and bless the Lord you people of His choice; stand up and bless the Lord, your God, with heart and soul and voice.

Chapter 6

Hebrew Meaning of Praise

Psalm 47:7 teaches us to sing praises with understanding.

Let's look now at the seven Hebrew meanings for the word 'Praise'. This will increase our understanding and ability to Praise God more effectively. We truly praise God when we fulfill all of His Word.

1. Yadah -
Throw out the hands.

> "Lift up your hands in the sanctuary,
> and bless the Lord."
> Psalm 134:2

2. Taldah -
Vocal expression of thanksgiving.

> "O Lord, open Thou my lips,

and my mouth shall shew forth Thy praise."

Psalm 51:15

"O come, let us sing unto the Lord:
Let us make a joyful noise to
the rock of our salvation. Let us come
before His presence with thanksgiving,
and make a joyful noise unto Him with psalms.

Psalm 95:1,2

3.   Halal -
To be clear, boast, rave, celebrate, to be clamorously foolish.

"Praise ye the Lord.
Praise God in His sanctuary:
praise Him in the firmament of His power.
Praise Him for his mighty acts:
praise Him according to His excellent greatness.
Praise Him with the sound of the trumpet:
praise Him with the psaltery and harp.
Praise Him with the timbrel and dance:
praise Him with stringed instruments and organs.
Praise Him upon the loud cymbals:
praise Him upon the high sounding cymbals.
Let every thing that hath breath praise the Lord.
Praise ye the Lord."

Psalm 150

4. Shabach -
To shout, praise loudly.

> "O bless our God, ye people,
> and make the voice of His praise to be heard."
>
> Psalm 66:8

5. Barak -
Bless or bow down in reverent expectation.

> "Great is the Lord,
> and greatly to be praised in the city of our God,
> in the mountain of His holiness."
>
> Psalm 48:1

6. Zamar -
To touch strings and instruments, clapping hands.

> "O clap your hands, all ye people;
> shout unto God with the voice of triumph."
>
> Psalm 47:1

7. Tehillah -
To sing Hallelujah.

> "Sing praises to God, sing praises:
> sing praises unto our King, sing praises."
> Psalm 47:6

8.   Hallelujah -
One universal word meaning - Praise the Lord, or let us praise the Lord. In every language Hallelujah means 'Praise The Lord'!

Remember ...
> "... in the last days men will be unthankful..."'

2 Timothy 3:1 and 2

Praising God is showing forth our gratitude to our Creator, thanking Him. Let's not fall into the unthankful group.

Psalm 9:1 "I will praise Thee, O Lord, with my whole heart; I will shew forth all Thy marvelous works."

PRAISE IS FAITH AT WORK

Have you ever noticed the way God multiplies your faith when you begin praising Him? There are times when it is more important to praise God than to pray to Him a prayer of intercession. Praise lifts your eyes from your circumstances to your almighty Father who is ruler over all.

Praise lifts your eyes from the battle to the victory, for Christ is already the Victor, and though we do not yet see all things under His feet, they are there (see Hebrews 2:8 and Ephesians 1:22) in a divine reality.

When you need faith, there are two steps to take: go to God's Word, and begin praising Him. These two go together as naturally as hydrogen and oxygen together make water. Stop worrying or fearing and start praising. Do you need faith? THEN PRAISE THE LORD by declaring His word back to Him with a joyful and thankful heart.

Chapter 7

Praise Is Worship

If you want a new fountain of joy to spring up in the soil of your heart, start praising God. God's Word tells us that He places a new song in our hearts. If we are not singing Christians we are disappointing God. God wants His people to begin worship by approaching Him with praise: "Enter into His gates with thanksgiving, and into His courts with praise" (Psalm 100:4). All the graces of the Holy Spirit grow much better in a happy heart.

In each crisis, when God meets the soul in a new way, He brings unspeakable joy, new peace and a touch of His glory. Praise should be as inevitable as water flowing from a fountain. Whenever the clouds of darkness begin to hide God's loving face, praise is the quickest way through to His glorious light again. Is your spiritual life lacking in joy? Be sure that there is no hidden sin, and then just start praising God. PRAISE THE LORD!

Have you ever realized that God's answers to your prayers are at times delayed by your lack of praise to God? Have you seen God remove insurmountable difficulties and obstructions in answer to praise? Did you know that you can often cause Satan to flee faster through praise than in any other way? Have you experienced the effectiveness of praise and fasting? Did you know that bodies have been healed, demons have been cast out and peace restored to troubled hearts by simply praising the Lord?

Have you ever deliberately gone into an impossible situation with the weapon of praise to God, and watched God perform the miracle? Oh hungry-hearted, struggling child of God, oh saint of God, battling the forces of darkness, oh interceding prayer-warrior, this may be God's message to you! Look up just now and begin to praise God. PRAISE THE LORD!

Perhaps it is seldom that God would have us do nothing but ask and intercede. It may also be true that God would seldom have us spend a protracted time in nothing but praise to God. There is scarcely a spiritual conflict into which we enter without some measure of prayer; but how often do we, like Judah under Jehoshaphat (2 Chronicles 20:20-21) march into battle doing nothing but believing and praising? Oh, my Christian brothers and sisters, let us begin to praise God more. Praise changes situations, and praise will transform you!

There is, at times, a deep sacrifice in praise. There are times when we must praise God though tears might be in our eyes. There are times when everything that could go wrong has gone wrong and all we can say is "Praise to the Lord" anyway. There is no sweeter music under heaven; there is no more fragrant perfume than that which arises from a life of suffering which is nevertheless filled with praise.

No doubt today you are facing situations not of your own choosing. Can you look up just now out of your Gethsemane (your place of

temptation and trial) and still say, 'PRAISE THE LORD!'
Remember in John 10:10 we read that the thief comes to steal, kill and destroy, but Jesus has come to give us God's blessings and life in all its abundance. Everything in your life right now is subject to change. God's will for your life is that it changes for the better. Praise is the language of faith and faith is the language of heaven. Don't quit, don't give up, remember when all else fails, Praise prevails.

PRAISE IS THE LANGUAGE OF HEAVEN

Praise will sweeten and hallow all that it touches. Praise will kindle a new faith. Praise will fan the sparks of your smouldering love into a flaming love for God. Praise will start the joy bells ringing in your soul; you will soon have all heaven joining in on the chorus and you will have a touch of heaven in your heart. Praise will pierce through the darkness, dynamite away longstanding obstructions, and strike terror in the heart of Satan.

In the past we have praised God a little and occasionally; now let us praise Him more and more. Look up to heaven just now and praise your mighty Redeemer. Praise Him for His love and faithfulness; praise Him for His power and goodness. He is worthy of all praise; let us praise Him now! PRAISE THE LORD!

He is worthy to be praised,
He is worthy to be praised,
He's the Lord of Glory,
The Ancient of Days:
He is worthy to be praised.

PRAISING GOD MAKES YOU TRIUMPH IN BATTLE

Prayer and praise are the two steps by which the army of the Lord marches forward. As surely as soldiers march always "Left, right, left, right" so we must keep our praising as up-to-date as our praying – if we want to advance for God.

We are all in danger of neglecting prayer, and we are perhaps all in even greater danger of neglecting praise. Many a prayer meeting would come to new life and power, if men began to praise the Lord.

If there is anything that is a better gauge of the Spiritual life than Prayer life, it is the Praise life. Satan fears prayer. If there is anything Satan fears more than prayer, it is praise.

God Waits to Hear the Voices of His Children.

You may say, "I don't have a great singing voice, I can't keep in tune." Don't let that deter you. God is not looking for that skilled, flawless voice. If you have a talent like that then use it for God's glory, and if you don't, God is still looking for the heart that will sing to Him, express His praise and make a joyful sound unto the Lord.

It is the sweetest of music to His ear. If there is anything He delights to hear more than the voice of prayer and petition, it is the voice of praise and adoration.

PRAYER ADDS ITS SWEET PERFUME TO THE CHRISTIAN'S LIFE

Praise adds a sweet fragrance to prayer.

If there is anything that makes the Christian's life even more fragrant, it is praise. It is not a question of prayer or praise – we must keep the two together. We are to pray without ceasing, and much time also should be given to praise (Luke 21:36; 1 Thessalonians 5:17; Hebrews 13:12-15).

PRAISE MAKES THE SOUL BEAUTIFUL

It is perhaps the most heavenly activity in which the soul can engage. A life filled with praise becomes almost angelic. Praise, thanksgiving, love, adoration – these make life radiant.

THE HOLY SPIRIT SHINES THROUGH THE CHRISTIAN'S LIFE THAT IS SATURATED WITH PRAISE

The Shekinah glory of God marks a life that rejoices evermore, in everything gives thanks, and radiates pure love for God and others (1 Thessalonians 5:16-18; Romans 5:5).

Praise adds sweetness to the voice; praise adds loveliness to the soul. Praise fills the life with song, the heart with joy and adds graciousness to all life. Praise clothes with heaven's beauty.

Praise Report 3

Epilepsy Healed through Praise
- By Pauline Weeks -

I want to share my testimony on how the Power of Praise and putting it's principles to work changed my life. I became epileptic in my mid forties. After having a seizure I visited my local doctor who diagnosed me with epilepsy. This condition became traumatic as it progressed. The epilepsy had possibly been caused by an accident, when as a young child I suffered a major injury to my skull and brain after a nurse accidentally dropped me on my head on a concrete floor. As a result of this accident I spent many months hospitalised as a baby.

After becoming epileptic, I suffered grand-mal seizures for seven years. These seizures became very distressing for my family as they could be set off without warning in any place at any time. My family was constantly worried about me and my doctor's report meant I had to surrender my driver's license due to my deteriorating condition. I was now without a license and my quality of life was decreasing, and I was becoming quite anxious about my future.

Under the care of a Neuro-specialist, my condition was managed with medication, which I was told I would have to take for the rest of my life. The drug I was given did manage the seizures, but gave me bad side effects. I stopped taking them occasionally to give myself a break, but always the grand-mal seizures took over again. At that time I was seeking the Lord more deeply. I needed more of Him to cope with my increasing stress, though I didn't ask for healing in my prayer time. One morning, I cried out to God, "Please help me" I was desperate! Suddenly while still on my knees I felt His presence all around me and I was baptized in the Holy Spirit. Soon after that I was bold enough to remind Jesus that He had healed the epileptic boy in Matthew 17:15-18. I asked Him to heal me too. I began to praise Him for His loving kindness and believed the word in Exodus 15:26 "I am the Lord your healer". It was enough for me. I was ecstatic with joy! Dancing around the dining table I praised and worshipped the Lord. I stopped the medication and have never had a seizure since.

Since I have received my healing, I reapplied for my driver's license with permission from my Doctor, who though unable to explain it, after extensive medical examinations, gave me the 'all clear' letter for the police to have my license reinstated. At first I was on a year to year probational license, but now I am once again on a full open license.

As I write this testimony I praise God that I have now been free from epilepsy, never having suffered another seizure for the last 28 years. Praise God! I serve a living God who heals today and has restored my health and quality of life. Jesus is Jehovah! My Healer, Provider, my Shephard, Victory and my Peace. Hallelujah! Praise God forevermore!

PRAISE OPENS THE GATES TO BLESSING

Praise needs to be put literally first in prayer. It is significant that in the future prophesied glory, when our walls are "Salvation", our gates will be "Praise" (Isaiah 60:18). "Enter into His gates with thanksgiving, and into His courts with praise" Psalm 100:4.

There is no more worthy entrance into the presence of God than the entrance of praise. Praise opens the gates to blessing. Praise opens the way to the very heart of God.

"Oh that men would praise the Lord for His goodness and for His wonderful works to the children of men! And let them sacrifice the sacrifices of thanksgiving, and declare His works with rejoicing." Psalm 107:21-22.

PRAISE MULTIPLIES THE PRESENCE AND POWER OF THE LORD

It is a secret of the blessed life – that praise not merely adds blessing, it multiplies every blessing of God. Praise fills the life with an atmosphere of heaven.

There are times when it is not easy to praise. Those are the times we need to praise anyway. "By Him ... let us offer the sacrifice of praise to God continually, that is, the fruit of our lips, giving thanks to His name." Hebrews 13:15. When you begin to praise, the disquiet of your heart and the restlessness and fear of your soul begins to disappear like fog before sunshine.

When you begin to praise, peace is blessedly multiplied within your soul. When you begin to praise, sorrow turns to joy.

When you begin to praise, grumbling and criticism wither to the roots, the breath of heaven blows the clouds away, and you feel so clean and new again. When you begin to praise, Satan turns in terror and soon flees away.

Praising God opens your heart to God, and to all His heavenly influences.

Praising God welcomes the Holy Spirit and gives Him the right of way in your life. Praising God lifts you above the trivial accusations of Satan. Praising God reduces your problem from mountains into hills of blessing!

Praising God gives you the eagle's vision, and by the eye of faith you see the victory ahead! Praising God multiplies your faith and fills you with joy and peace in believing (Romans 15:13).
Praising God seems to fill you with the very faith of God and strengthen you with the power of the Holy Ghost. Praising God changes you – and changes the situation before you! Praising God opens the way to miracles.

Praising God makes you triumphant in the battle. Praising God brings to your aid all the resources of heaven. The angels of God recognise the sound of praise and rush to your side to win the victory for God. Praising God brings the shout of victory in the midst of the battle.

Praising God ambushes the devil. In the time of Jehoshaphat when the King and his people humbled themselves and sought God's

PRAISE REPORT 3

face, He put His Spirit on an unknown Levite and gave them a message of hope. They believed the promise of God and marched into battle – with singers praising God in front of the battle troops. "And when they began to sing and to praise, the Lord set ambushments." 2 Chronicles 20:22.

Praise sets an ambush for the devil. No wonder he flees at the sound of praise! When Israel praised God, the walls of Jericho fell down. When Paul and Silas prayed and sang praises unto God, the Lord shook open the doors of the jail of Philippi (Acts 16:23-34).

> And when YOU begin to praise the Lord –
> New victories will happen for YOU!
> This was the secret that David learned
> and we all need to learn it over and over.

Hear David testify, "I will bless the Lord at all times: His praise shall continually be in my mouth" Psalm 34:1. "My tongue shall speak of . . . Thy praise all the day."

Psalm 35:28. "Let my mouth be filled with Thy praise . . . all the day".

Psalm 71:8. "Who can shew forth all His praise?"

Psalm 106:2. "I will hope continually, and will yet praise Thee more and more . . . I will go in the strength of the Lord".

Psalm 71:14,16. Can you see why David was a man after God's own heart? (See Acts 13:22).

Let us make this year, a year of praise. Begin by making this day a day of praise. Begin by filling your heart with God's praises wherever you go. Begin by praising the Lord first thing each morning. Begin by praising God every time you feel tempted to doubt, to fear, to worry, to criticise, to yield to any kind of temptation. Praise fills you with faith and power. Praise clothes you with heaven's beauty. Praise opens the gates to blessing. Praise wins the battle for God.

Psalm 146:1-2. "Praise the Lord, O my soul. While I live will I praise the Lord; I will sing praises unto my God." Because Thy loving kindness is better than life, my lips shall praise Thee. Thus will I bless Thee while I live: I will lift up my hands in Thy name." Psalm 63:3-4. I shall praise the Lord "with all that is within me" including the beautiful act of lifting up my hands in praise to my Lord! "Lift up your hands in the sanctuary, and bless the Lord" Psalm 134:2.

I know that in public worship, "all things are to be done decently and in order" 1 Corinthians 14:40. But there is nothing indecent or disorderly about praising Jesus "in the sanctuary" by lifting up our hands! Hallelujah, I shall do it! I know that lifting up my hands in prayer, praise and worship is God's desire for me.

"I will bless the Lord at all times" even by the lifting up of my hands unto Him. Hallelujah!

Chapter 8

Psalm 107

❧ ☙

LET US TAKE A LOOK AT PSALM 107
AND RECEIVE INSTRUCTION FROM GOD'S WORD

Psalm 107

"O Give thanks unto the Lord, for He is good:
for His mercy endureth forever.
Let the redeemed of the Lord say so,
whom He hath redeemed from the hand of the enemy;
And gathered them out of the lands,
from the east, and from the west,
from the north and from the south.
They wandered in the wilderness in a solitary way;
they found no city to dwell in.
Hungry and thirsty, their soul fainted in them.
Then they cried unto the Lord in their trouble,
and He delivered them out of their distresses.
And He held them forth by the right way,
that they might go to a city of habitation.

Oh that men would praise the Lord for His goodness,

and for His wonderful works to the children of men!

For He satisfieth the longing soul,
and filleth the hungry soul with goodness.
Such as sit in darkness and in the shadow of death,
being bound in affliction and iron;
Because they rebelled against the words of God,
and condemned the counsel of the most High:
Therefore He brought down their heart with labour;
they fell down, and there was none to help.
Then they cried unto the Lord in their trouble,
and He saved them out of their distresses.
He brought them out of darkness and the shadow of death,
and brake their bands in sunder.
Oh that men would praise the Lord for His goodness,
and for His wonderful works to the children of men!

For He hath broken the gates of brass,
and cut the bars of iron in sunder.
Fools because of their transgression,
and because of their iniquities, are afflicted.
Their soul abhorreth all manner of meat;
and they draw near unto the gates of death.
Then they cry unto the Lord in their trouble,
and He saveth them out of their distresses.
He sent His Word, and healed them,
and delivered them from their destructions.

Oh that men would praise the Lord for His goodness,
and for His wonderful works to the children of men!
And let them sacrifice the sacrifices of thanksgiving,
and declare His works with rejoicing.

PSALM 107

They that go down to the sea in ships,
 that do business in great waters;
 These see the works of the Lord,
 and His wonders in the deep.
For He commandeth, and raiseth the stormy wind,
 which lifteth up the waves thereof.
 They mount up to the heaven,
 they go down again to the depths:
 their soul is melted because of trouble.
They reel to and fro, and stagger like a drunken man,
 and are at their wit's end.

Then they cry unto the Lord in their trouble,
 and He bringeth them out of their distresses.
He maketh the storm a calm, so that the waves thereof are still.
 Then are they glad because they be quiet;
 so He bringeth them unto their desired haven.

Oh that men would praise the Lord for His goodness,
 and for His wonderful works to the children of men!

Let them exalt Him also in the congregation of the people,
 and praise Him in the assembly of the elders.
 He turneth rivers into a wilderness,
 and the watersprings into dry ground;
 A fruitful land into barrenness,
 for the wickedness of them that dwell therein.
 He turneth the wilderness into a standing water,
 and dry ground into watersprings.
 And there He maketh the hungry to dwell,
 that they may prepare a city for habitation;
 And sow the fields, and plant vineyards,

which may yield fruits of increase.
He blesseth them also, so that they are multiplied greatly;
and suffereth not their cattle to decrease.
Again, they are minished and brought low through oppression,
affliction, and sorrow.
He poureth contempt upon princes,
and causeth them to wander in the wilderness,
where there is no way.
Yet setteth He the poor on high from affliction,
and maketh him families like a flock.
The righteous shall see it, and rejoice:
and all iniquity shall stop her mouth.
Who is wise, and will observe these things,
even they shall understand the loving kindness of the Lord."

"Oh that men would praise the Lord..."

Here we see the heart cry of God. Oh that men would praise the Lord -Over and over again these words are repeated. The Psalm ends with verse 43,

"Whoso is wise, and will observe these things, even they shall understand the loving kindness of the Lord."

If you are wise, you will Praise the Lord.

FAITH WORK

1. What should people do?

_____

_____

_____

2. What would a wise man do?

_____

_____

_____

3. Look up and write out the scripture of Isaiah 1:19.

_____

_____

_____

Chapter 9

Benefits of Praise

1 Peter 2:9 (NKJV)

"But you are a chosen generation, a royal priesthood, a holy nation, His own special people, that you may proclaim the praises of Him who called you out of darkness into His marvellous light".

I have listed many of the benefits of praise throughout this book. I am sure that this side of eternity, we will never fully be able to comprehend all the great virtues of magnifying the Lord, but one of the greatest benefits of praise is that you're obeying God. It pays to be obedient to the Lord. There is great blessing in obedience.

Isaiah 1:19 "If ye be willing and obedient, ye shall eat the good of the land."

The Bible says to obey is better than sacrifice.

1 Samuel 15:22 "...Has the LORD as great delight in burnt offerings and sacrifices, as in obeying the voice of the LORD? Behold, to obey is better than sacrifice, and to hearken than the fat of rams."

I have outlined below a further nine benefits of praise:

1.   Praise will give us the Victory.

1 Corinthians 15:57 "But thanks be to God, which giveth us the victory through our Lord Jesus Christ."

2.   Praise will bring Healing.

Psalm 42:11 "...for I shall yet praise Him, who is the health of my Countenance...".

Proverbs 17:22 "...A merry heart doeth good like a medicine..."

3.   Praise brings the Presence of God.

Psalm 22:3   "But Thou art holy, O Thou that inhabitest the praises of Israel."

2 Chronicles 5:13,14 "It came even to pass, as the trumpeters and singers were as one, to make one sound to be heard in praising and thanking the Lord; and when they lifted up their voice with the trumpets and cymbals and instruments of music, and praised the Lord, saying, For He is good; for His mercy endureth forever: that then the house was filled with a cloud, even the house of the Lord; so that the priests could not stand to minister by reason of the cloud: for the glory of the Lord had filled the house of God."

4.   Praise brings the fullness of Joy.

Psalm 16:11 "Thou wilt shew me the path of life: in Thy presence is fullness of joy; at Thy right hand there are pleasures for evermore."

5. Praise brings Strength.

Matthew 21:16 "And He said unto Him, "Hearest Thou what these say?" And Jesus saith unto them, Yea; have ye never read, out of the mouth of babes and sucklings thou has perfected praise?"

Psalm 8:2 "Out of the mouth of babes and sucklings hast Thou ordained strength because of Thine enemies, that Thou mightest still the enemy and the avenger."

The word `strength' in the Hebrew means: force, majesty, security, praise, boldness, loud, might, power, strong.

Nehemiah 8:10 "...for the joy of the Lord is your strength."

Psalm 71:14 and 16 "But I will hope continually, and will yet praise Thee more and more. I will go in the strength of the Lord God: I will make mention of Thy righteousness, even of Thine only."

6. Praise brings Protection.

Psalm 5:11,12 "But let all those that put their trust in Thee rejoice: let them ever shout for joy, because Thou defendest them: let them also that love Thy name be joyful in Thee. For Thou, Lord, wilt bless the righteous, with favour wilt Thou compass him as with a shield."

Psalm 18:3 "I will call upon the Lord, Who is worthy to be praised: so shall I be saved from mine enemies."

7.   Praise brings Provision.

Philippians 4:6 "Be anxious for nothing, but in everything by prayer and supplication, with thanksgiving, let your requests be made known to God."

Psalm 35:27   "Let them shout for joy, and be glad, that favour My righteous cause: yea, let them say continually, Let the Lord be magnified, which hath pleasure in the prosperity of His servant."

Psalm 16:11 "Thou wilt show me the path of life: in Thy presence is fullness of joy; at Thy right hand there are pleasures for evermore."

8.   Praise brings Peace.

Colossians 3:15,16   "And let the peace of God rule in your hearts, to the which also ye are called in one body; and be ye thankful. Let the Word of Christ dwell in you richly in all wisdom, teaching and admonishing one another in psalms and hymns and spiritual songs, singing with grace in your hearts to the Lord."

Isaiah 26:3 "Thou wilt keep him in perfect peace, whose mind is stayed on Thee: because he trusteth in Thee."

9.   Praise brings Deliverance.

Psalm 18:3 "I will call upon the Lord, Who is worthy to be praised: so shall I be saved from mine enemies."
When all else fails, Praise prevails!!

Human persuasion, begging with tears, and other emotional demands often fail to produce anticipated results. Praise, however, never fails to bring God's response to us in our needs and circumstances.

Why does Praise prevail? Because God inhabits our Praises! Remember, Praise is the language of faith, and faith is the Victory. Therefore, Praise is the language of heaven.

PRAISE THOUGHTS

1. Praise, like sunlight, helps all things to grow.
2. We can never praise Jesus too much.
3. God gives blessings to us so we can give glory to Him.
4. Be sure to concentrate on your blessings – not your distresses.
5. A heart of praise and love shows others just what Jesus can do in the lives of men.
6. Praise is the soil in which joy thrives.
7. God's work of creating is done; our work of praising has just begun.
8. Praise is good medicine to take daily for depression.
9. A tongue of praise has no time to gossip.
10. If you find yourself wearing a spirit of heaviness (depression), put on a garment of praise.
11. When all else fails, Praise prevails.
12. Don't quit, don't you ever quit!
    Praise will bring you through the darkest night.
13. "Let every thing that has breath, Praise the Lord."
14. If you can breathe, you can Praise.

Praise Report 4

The Miracle of the Weather

☙ ❧

Mark 4:39 "And He arose, and rebuked the wind, and said unto the sea, Peace, be still. And the wind ceased, and there was a great calm. And He said unto them, Why are ye so fearful? How is it that ye have no faith? And they feared exceedingly. And said one to another, What manner of Man is this, that even the wind and the sea obey Him?"

I recall a crusade in India by members of our congregation during which many miracles took place, the sick were healed and many thousands gave their hearts to Jesus. God moved strongly in our favour during our time there, but that was not what the circumstances suggested at the outset.

Let me tell you about the miracle of the weather. I was due to leave Brisbane on a Saturday in time to attend the open-air meetings in Kakinada on the Monday, when I received a call from our leader in India, Dr Raj Kiran. His voice broke when he told me that major storms were forecast for the Kakinada region. All the headlines in India's newspapers carried warnings about terrible storms. Raj was justifiably upset. Over seventy thousand dollars had been spent on preparations for the outreach, and three months of hard work had gone into the planning of the forthcoming events.

Sensing his dismay at the possibility of a washed-out event or, even worse, a cancellation of our outreach, I turned to God for the answer. God is always available to us, especially in emergencies. Then I asked Raj to hold the phone out of the window and I spoke with Godly authority: "Rain, I command you to cease in Jesus' name!" Hebrews 1:14 teaches us this: "What are the angels, then? They are spirits who serve God and are sent by Him to help those who are to receive salvation." I asked God to take all the rain destined for Kakinada during our meetings and redirect the clouds to our drought-stricken Brisbane. Australia had been suffering from a crippling drought at that time and there was no end to the drought in sight. Then I praised God for His greatness and that His angels would move those rain-filled clouds down to Brisbane, Australia.

On the aeroplane to Singapore en-route to India, our friendly flight attendant informed me that she was from Kakinada and that a terrible monsoon was heading for the city, having already caused chaos in Chenai, a neighbouring region. I chose to ignore her words of warning, and instead, praised God that He had heard and answered my prayer. I asked God for His favour during our gatherings.

God answered my praise-filled prayers in a mighty and miraculous way. During our four main open-air meetings at night, not a single drop of rain fell! Brisbane, to the contrary, had torrential rain and the drought was finally broken. Our church in Bald Hills witnessed this miracle take place that week. This was truly thanks to God's favour, purpose and destiny.

PRAISE REPORT 4

During our last evening in Kakinada, it was reported that the city itself received rain, yet where we were in the large open-air meeting place where the thousands had gathered to worship God, not a drop fell and all enjoyed a dry and beautiful evening. The power of praise and the magnitude of miracle upon miracle astounded even the pastors in the city. During these outreach meetings, thousands of people streamed into the open-air arenas to hear the Word of God. Our merciful and powerful Father ordained the weather to stay clear, keeping the rain clouds at bay. In a town of four hundred and fifty thousand people, an incredible two hundred and fifty thousand souls were saved! Through praise and confidence in God's Word, the spiritual war was won. Glory to God in the highest!

CHAPTER 10

SPIRITUAL WARFARE

Ephesians 6:10-19 says, "Finally, my brethren, be strong in the Lord, and in the power of His might. Put on the whole armour of God, that ye may be able to stand against the wiles of the devil. For we wrestle not against flesh and blood, but against principalities, against powers, against the rulers of the darkness of this world, against spiritual wickedness in high places. Wherefore take unto you the whole armour of God, that ye may be able to withstand in the evil day, and having done all, to stand. Stand therefore, having your loins girt about with truth, and having on the breastplate of righteousness; and your feet shod with the preparation of the gospel of peace; Above all, taking the shield of faith, wherewith ye shall be able to quench all the fiery darts of the wicked. And take the helmet of salvation, and the sword of the Spirit, which is the Word of God: praying always with all prayer and supplication in the Spirit, and watching thereunto with all perseverance and supplication for all saints; And for me, that utterance may be given unto me, that I may open my mouth boldly, to make known the mystery of the gospel."

The Word of God shows us here that we are involved in warfare.

We are warned to put on the whole armour of God. Satan is involved in this war because he wants to discredit God and destroy mankind. In John 10:10, Jesus describes Satan as a thief who comes to kill, steal and destroy. The word 'wiles' in the above Scripture refers to the military strategies of the devil. The Bible tells us our war is not against flesh and blood, but against the military strategies of the devil. The word 'wrestle' in the above scripture means to sing or vibrate.

Our God is a victorious, overcoming God. He is not a man that He should lie!
As we praise Him, He inhabits (moves into) our praises. Satan has to flee out of the presence of the almighty God. Spiritual warfare drives the presence of the evil one away from us. We must prepare ourselves for war daily by allowing the Holy Spirit to strengthen our inner man as we read God's Word and pray and sing in the Spirit. Warfare is for worshippers. As we sing in worship and praise our God, we effect defeat over Satan. God's army is a singing musical army of people who love to praise Him with their whole heart. Our lifestyle of praise and worship cuts through the enemy lines wherever they may be. As praisers, we will find the enemy retreating against the invisible weapons of Spirit-filled praise and worship to God. The battleground is in our mind and in the air (see Ephesians 2:2 and 2 Corinthians 10: 4-5).

The 'air' refers to the atmosphere which surrounds planet earth which is conducive to carrying sound. As we fill the air with our loud voices of high praise, we see in Psalm 22:3 that we surround ourselves with the presence of God. God's presence is in our heart, where He dwells. We take of His presence and sing it into the circumstances surrounding our lives. God's presence dispels all that is not of God. It is wonderful that God lives in the believer and that we have everlasting life. It is powerful to let that life loose in you, then God can be all that He is and do all that He can do. These words of praise pass through our mind and in this way our mind is renewed by the Word of God. Our ears hear the words as they pass through the air, then they are picked up and registered once again in our mind. From there the Word goes down into our spirit and faith comes to us by hearing the Word of God. The weapons of our warfare are not carnal, but are mighty through God to the pulling down of strongholds - the total destruction of all of Satan's strongholds over our life, mind or circumstances. We use the power of the Word in warfare. Ecclesiastes 8:4 says, "Where the Word of a King is, there is power." Remember, according to Hebrews 4:12, "...the Word of God is quick and powerful, sharper than any two-edged sword."

(For further teaching on this topic, obtain a copy of *Spiritual Warfare* by Dr. Shaun Marler).

WORSHIP

When we open our heart in worship we are saying to God, "Lord, I throw open every door of my life, come into every part of me and fill me. You are the creator, I am the created."

David did two things to make sure God's presence remained in Jerusalem. First, he prepared a place for God's presence by constructing a tabernacle without walls or a veil. Second, he did something special once the Levites arrived at the tabernacle and set the ark of the covenant in place. He created a "living" mercy seat of worship in the tabernacle, so God would be pleased to sit and remain in that humble sanctuary.

David learned a vital secret somewhere in the process of bringing God's presence into Jerusalem. He learned that if you want to keep that blue flame there, somebody has to tend the fire! "Do you mean we have to throw logs on the fire?" No, you don't fuel that blue flame of God's shekinah presence with earthly fuel. You fuel it through sacrificial worship. We have no right to call for the fire of God unless we are willing to be the fuel of God.

David was simply following the heavenly pattern Moses had received for the mercy seat: "And you shall make two cherubim of gold; of hammered work you shall make them at the two ends of the mercy seat. Make one cherub at one end, and the other cherub at the other end; you shall make the cherubim at the two ends of it of the one piece with the mercy seat. And the cherubim shall stretch out their wings above, covering the mercy seat with their wings, and they shall face one another; the faces of the cherubim shall be toward the mercy seat" (Exodus 25: 18-20 NKJV). It was their perpetual bondage of the Children of Israel that brought Egypt to the final and worst plague of all. The time for the divine exodus was near, and justice would wait no longer. The Lord spoke to Moses and commanded every Israelite household in Goshen (the despised territory of shepherds inhabited by the Israelites), to slay a lamb without blemish and to apply its blood with a bunch of hyssop to the door posts and lintels of their homes. Their orders were simple: Stay in the house and stay under the blood. (See Exodus 12: 1-22).

The Bible declares we overcome the evil one by the blood of the Lamb and the word of our testimony (Revelation 12:11). Our testimony should always be full of praise and thanksgiving, exalting the Word, declaring the exceeding great and precious promises of God. Declaring everything that God is and all that He has done for us. Our testimony is who we are in Christ and who Christ is in us.

Never forget:
1. God can do what He says He can do.
2. God has what He says He has.
3. God is Who He says He is.

You can do what God says you can do.
You have what God says you have.
You are who God says you are.

FAITH WORK

Write out Matthew 21:16

_____
_____
_____
_____
_____

Praise here can also be interchanged with the word, strength.

Write out Psalm 8:2

_____
_____
_____
_____
_____

What does 'strength' or 'praise' here mean in the Hebrew?

_____
_____
_____
_____
_____

Words of praise being issued forth from your mouth are a mighty force for the spirit realm to destroy the works of darkness.

Chapter 11

Praise In Warfare

In the Bible, praise was used many times and today it still is a mighty weapon in warfare. Through the power of praise we come against the kingdom of darkness, reinforcing the victory that Christ has won for us. Let's look at three very good examples of this in the Word.

GIDEON

In the sixth chapter of the book of Judges we see Israel once again in trouble. They had done evil in the sight of the Lord and He had delivered them into the hands of the Midianites. When they began to call on the Lord, He sent them Gideon to deliver them.

Gideon did a great job of raising an army of thirty-two thousand soldiers, but the Lord said, "The people that are with thee are too many for Me to give the Midianites into their hands, lest Israel vaunt themselves against Me, saying 'Mine own hand hath saved me'." Judges 7:2.

By the time the Lord weeded out the ones that shouldn't have been in His army, there were only three hundred men left. These three hundred had to run into the enemy camp holding a lamp in one hand and a trumpet in the other and shout, "The sword of the Lord, and of Gideon."

Suddenly we realise that God's ways of battle and ours are very different. As these men ran into the enemy camp with words of praise in their mouths, the Lord caused the enemy to rise up and kill one another, showing Israel that God does not need our fleshly weapons... just people that will praise Him in the face of the enemy.

JEHOSHAPHAT

In 2 Chronicles 20 we see the second instance of victory through praise.

Israel was in trouble again. A great multitude of Moabites and Ammonites came against them and Jehoshaphat was fearful. Then he took three steps that led to total victory:

1. He set himself to seek the Lord. (Verse 3)
2. He proclaimed a fast throughout all Judah. (Verse 3)
3. He appointed singers unto the Lord, and they praised the Lord in the beauty of holiness as they went out before the army. (Verse 21).

"And when they began to sing and praise, the Lord set ambushments against the Ammonites, Moabites and children of Mount Seir, which were come against Judah; and they were smitten...

everyone helped to destroy another." (Verses 22 & 23).
Once again Israel did not even have to pick up a weapon. God won the battle for them as He promised in verse 17. All He needed was people who would praise Him.

PAUL AND SILAS

In Acts 16:18 we see Paul and Silas casting a demon out of a young woman. Her masters caught Paul and Silas and threw them into prison, where they were beaten. These two men of God could have become very discouraged and quit the ministry. In the natural, they had absolutely nothing to be happy about.

Like Israel of old they were surrounded by their enemies whose wish was to be rid of them. They had no way of saving themselves.

So at midnight (Verse 25), "Paul and Silas prayed and sang praises unto God... And suddenly there was a great earthquake, so that the foundations of the prison were shaken: and immediately all the doors were opened, and everyone's bands were loosed." As a result the jailer was saved and they were set free.

That is real praise power. This power is available for those who know God and have spent time in His presence and are walking according to His word. When these people begin to pray and praise, the power of God goes into operation and great victories are won!

Many Christians are faithful to pray and seek the Lord when in spiritual warfare. Some even will fast to see the bonds of the enemy broken, but many fall short of the victory because they do not enter into praise and worship.

Faith in our heart will cause us to praise even before we see the answer. Unbelief will hinder praise. So then, we are to begin to offer the sacrifice of praise. As we begin to glorify God for His faithfulness... His power... His love toward us... His promises to us... the victories we have had in the past... the power of the blood of Jesus and the anointing of the Spirit... then the faith in our heart pours forth and the power of God begins to move for us.

OUR DOMINION

There is power and authority, but there is also dominion. Dominion is the highest form of rule.

We see in Genesis 1:28 that when God created Adam and Eve, He gave them dominion over all the earth. When they sinned, they lost the dominion that God had given to them. In other words, they handed that dominion over to Satan and he became the ruler of this world and also the ruler of man. Satan reminded Christ of this when he tempted Him and said: "All this power will I give Thee, and the glory of them; for that is delivered unto me; and to whomsoever I will, I give it." Luke 4:6.

The only catch was that Jesus had to worship Satan to get what he offered. Jesus did not come to earth to submit Himself to Satan, but to defeat him.

Jesus came to earth to redeem us through His precious blood, and once again to restore that dominion to us.

If you don't have dominion over Satan, then he will have dominion

over you. He will dominate your spirit, soul and body. You will be weak and he will keep you in bondage.
There are many who are in chains because of spiritual bondage. But there are also many who have been set free, and in this warfare they have dominion and are exercising it.

Satan is the prince, or god, of this world, but the spiritually alive man has dominion over him (Genesis 3:15). It is very important to have dominion over the devil so as to be free, and to stay free, from his power. Only when you are free and have dominion over Satan can you help to get others free.

Matthew 12:28-29 says: "If I cast out devils by the Spirit of God, then the kingdom of God is come unto you. Or else how can one enter into a strong man's house and spoil his goods, except he first bind the strong man? And then he will spoil his house."

Satan was that strong man. Jesus, the source of power, bound him. Jesus took away Satan's power and gave it to the church. He gave us dominion over the world...the flesh...and the devil!

As we praise God, declaring the victory, we establish that victory in the spiritual or heavenly realms around our life. We affect the very atmosphere around us. We are, you are, more than a conqueror through the Lord Jesus Christ.

David prayed this prayer: "Order my steps in Thy Word, and let not any iniquity have dominion over me." (Psalms 119:133)

David knew that if the enemy got dominion over him through iniquity or sin, he would not have power with God. This is why we cannot be successful in spiritual warfare if we allow any sin or rebellion in any form to have dominion over us.

David knew he had to walk according to the Word and keep sin out of his life.

Paul said: "Sin shall not have dominion over me." (Romans 6:14). This New Testament giant learned the same lesson David had learned. We also have to learn this if we are going to be victorious.

You have dominion over the devil. Jesus said: "Behold, I give unto you power to tread on serpents and scorpions, and over all the power of the enemy; and nothing shall by any means hurt you." Luke 10:19.

Captivate those desires and those thoughts to which Satan is trying to get you to yield. Move into battle now. Take authority over him. Let him know that Jesus restored dominion to you at Calvary. God will be glorified, and you will be able to rejoice!

Remember, praise is power; a mighty force that releases God's ability to work on your behalf. Praise arrests with force the enemy and the powers of darkness that move against you. Out of the mouths of babes (new Christians), God has ordained praise and strength to come forth, to destroy the enemies' work, to defeat them and turn them back.

Chapter 12

Praying The Scriptures

One of the most powerful ways a believer can pray and praise, is to pray and praise the Word of God. This is how the early church prayed in Acts 4:23-31. We note how much they declared the promises of the Old Testament. As a result of this, God gave them a mighty visitation.

In Isaiah 43:26, God asks us to remind Him what He has said in His Word: "Put me in remembrance: let us plead together: declare thou, that thou mayest be justified."

In the earlier part of this century, the great Evangelical revival in Ireland featured believers praying the Scriptures. In her book written in 1648, Jeane Guyon spoke about praying the scriptures and entering into the presence of Christ that is in us. There is something about the Word of God in the heart and mouth that is life transforming.

Many years ago, in the Billy Graham crusades, businessmen learned to memorise the Scriptures like little children. They claimed that this transformed their lives. George Muller, the great man of faith who established the orphanages in Bristol, England, talked of spending half an hour meditating on one verse of Scripture and seeing amazing results because of this.

Reinhard Bonnke once shared how God spoke to him and said: "My Word in your mouth is as powerful as My Word in My mouth." He also said that, "In a miracle, five percent depends upon faith and ninety-five percent depends upon the Word". Brother Bonnke has been used mightily in great healing and deliverance crusades, especially in Africa, where hundreds of thousands turned to the Lord.

The greatest help in prayer is to know what the Bible says on any given subject, and then quote that in the presence of God Almighty. The believer who has learned to memorise, meditate upon, and speak the Word of God will become very powerful in the Lord. When you pray the Scriptures, you are praying the Will of God, because the Word of God is the Will of God. Pray out the Scriptures, apply them, and allow them to become real by making them alive at the time of prayer.

Indeed, a key for us to use against satanic attacks is Ephesians 6:17, which says, "And take...the sword of the Spirit, which is the word of God". In other words, the Spirit uses the Word as His sword and we should as well. As you declare the Word, the Holy Spirit will take that Word and destroy the works of Satan. This is how Jesus overcame satanic attacks. (See Matthew 4:1-11). Each of Satan's temptations contained the word "if". It was aimed to produce doubt.

In the first two temptations, Satan said, "If you are the Son of God...." This occurred shortly after Jesus was baptised by John in Jordan, when God the Father declared publicly "This is my beloved Son in whom I am well pleased" (Matthew 3:17 NKJV). Satan tempted Him concerning His Sonship.

The third temptation was not merely to make Jesus doubt but to try to cause Him to act in direct disobedience: "If you will fall down and worship me...." Satan wanted Him to break the greatest (the first) commandment.
This is the way Satan attacks us. He comes to us with doubt concerning our salvation. He comes with doubt concerning God's love, care and our acceptance into God's family. There are numerous attacks of the enemy. Jesus only used one weapon to defeat Satan: the "rhema" or spoken Word of God. As He quoted the Scriptures from the Old Testament, He countered each temptation with the same.

I encourage you every day to fill your heart and mind with the mighty promises of God contained in His word. Then to pray, speak and sing them forth, doing battle against principalities and powers. Then stand back and see the salvation of God, as He, through the power of your praise and the spoken word, moves into the midst of your circumstances. Remember, God creates the fruit of your lips. (Isaiah 57:19) Our words are the fruit produced by our lips. (Proverbs 18:20-21).

I have included for you here a portion of the scripture from the Old Testament, 2 Samuel Chapter 22. It's a song that King David sang to God, full of words to encourage himself when he faced adversity. David is known as the great psalmist of God. Read David's Song of Deliverance and be blessed:

2 Samuel 22

1 Then David spoke to the LORD the words of this song, on the day when the LORD had delivered him from the hand of all his enemies, and from the hand of Saul.
2 And he said:
"The LORD is my rock and my fortress and my deliverer;
3 The God of my strength, in whom I will trust;
My shield and the horn of my salvation,
My stronghold and my refuge;
My Savior, You save me from violence.
4 I will call upon the LORD, who is worthy to be praised;
So shall I be saved from my enemies.
5 When the waves of death surrounded me,
The floods of ungodliness made me afraid.
6 The sorrows of Sheol surrounded me;
The snares of death confronted me.
7 In my distress I called upon the LORD,
And cried out to my God;
He heard my voice from His temple,
And my cry entered His ears.

8 Then the earth shook and trembled;
The foundations of heaven quaked and were shaken,
Because He was angry.
9 Smoke went up from His nostrils,
And devouring fire from His mouth;
Coals were kindled by it.
10 He bowed the heavens also, and came down
With darkness under His feet.
11 He rode upon a cherub, and flew;

And He was seen upon the wings of the wind.
12 He made darkness canopies around Him,
Dark waters and thick clouds of the skies.
13 From the brightness before Him
Coals of fire were kindled.
14 The LORD thundered from heaven,
And the Most High uttered His voice.

15 He sent out arrows and scattered them;
Lightning bolts, and He vanquished them.
16 Then the channels of the sea were seen,
The foundations of the world were uncovered,
At the rebuke of the LORD,
At the blast of the breath of His nostrils.

17 He sent from above, He took me,
He drew me out of many waters.
18 He delivered me from my strong enemy,
From those who hated me;
For they were too strong for me.
19 They confronted me in the day of my calamity,
But the LORD was my support.
20 He also brought me out into a broad place;
He delivered me because He delighted in me.

21 The LORD rewarded me according to my righteousness;
According to the cleanness of my hands
He has recompensed me.
22 For I have kept the ways of the LORD,
And have not wickedly departed from my God.

23 For all His judgments were before me;
And as for His statutes, I did not depart from them.
24 I was also blameless before Him,
And I kept myself from my iniquity.
25 Therefore the LORD has recompensed me according to my righteousness,
According to my cleanness in His eyes.

26 With the merciful You will show Yourself merciful;
With a blameless man You will show Yourself blameless;
27 With the pure You will show Yourself pure;
And with the devious You will show Yourself shrewd.
28 You will save the humble people;
But Your eyes are on the haughty, that You may bring them down.

29 For You are my lamp, O LORD;
The LORD shall enlighten my darkness.
30 For by You I can run against a troop;
By my God I can leap over a wall.
31 As for God, His way is perfect;
The word of the LORD is proven;
He is a shield to all who trust in Him.

32 For who is God, except the LORD?
And who is a rock, except our God?
33 God is my strength and power,
And He makes my way perfect.
34 He makes my feet like the feet of deer,
And sets me on my high places.

35 He teaches my hands to make war,
So that my arms can bend a bow of bronze.

36 You have also given me the shield of Your salvation;
Your gentleness has made me great.
37 You enlarged my path under me;
So my feet did not slip.

38 "I have pursued my enemies and destroyed them;
Neither did I turn back again till they were destroyed.
39 And I have destroyed them and wounded them,
So that they could not rise;
They have fallen under my feet.
40 For You have armed me with strength for the battle;
You have subdued under me those who rose against me.
41 You have also given me the necks of my enemies,
So that I destroyed those who hated me.
42 They looked, but there was none to save;
Even to the LORD, but He did not answer them.
43 Then I beat them as fine as the dust of the earth;
I trod them like dirt in the streets,
And I spread them out.

44 You have also delivered me from the strivings of my people;
You have kept me as the head of the nations.
A people I have not known shall serve me.
45 The foreigners submit to me;
As soon as they hear, they obey me.
46 The foreigners fade away,
And come frightened from their hideouts.

47 The LORD lives!
Blessed be my Rock!
Let God be exalted,
The Rock of my salvation!
48 It is God who avenges me,
And subdues the peoples under me;
49 He delivers me from my enemies.
You also lift me up above those who rise against me;
You have delivered me from the violent man.
50 Therefore I will give thanks to You, O LORD, among the Gentiles,
And sing praises to Your name.

51 He is the tower of salvation to His king,
And shows mercy to His anointed,
To David and his descendants forevermore."

FAITH WORK

Scriptures to Meditate:

Jeremiah 29: 12
"Then shall you call upon Me, and you shall go and pray unto Me, and I will hearken unto you."

Jeremiah 29: 13
"And you shall seek Me and find Me, when you search for Me with all your heart."

Proverbs 8:17
"I love those who love Me, and those who seek Me early shall find Me."

Praise Report 5

Praise Brings Favour
-By Nathanael Marler-

I was recently holding revival meetings in South Australia. The first time I had spoken to the pastor we had cross communicated and I wrote down in my diary that the revival meetings were in Western Australia. I had booked the tickets in advance to get the cheaper deal from the airline. Three days from leaving I received a text message from a friend requesting the suburb where the meetings were to be held in Western Australia. He told me he had a friend who would be delighted to meet me in Western Australia. So I phoned the pastor and asked him the suburb, and to my surprise he said "It's the wrong state mate, it's South Australia!" I thought he was joking at first, because I had organised tickets and people for Western Australia. So I said to him "Well I might not be able to come mate, I might not be able to get on the plane". I was worried because I know the airline's policy on cheap tickets They are not flexible! You take it or leave it! The expensive tickets were flexible, but the cheap tickets are fixed firm.

I began to Praise God and thank him for his blessings and praise him for his goodness.

I phoned the airline and explained that I had made a mistake. The man who was serving me apologised and said "I'm sorry sir, those tickets are not flexible. It's company policy, we cannot change the cheaper tickets."

He then asked me again what my name was. "My name is Nathanael" I said. He then said "Like Nathanael the biblical name?" I replied "Yes". He went on to say "like a prophesying preacher Nathanael?" I said "Yes, that is exactly what I do and is the reason why I'm needing the tickets changed." He said to me "Well my name is Christian and I am a Christian and it's your lucky day".

He changed the tickets, got me on the plane and I did the meetings!

When I had left South Australia and boarded the airplane I noticed the plane was very full. I was stuffed down the rear of the plane. Just as I got my seat belt on, this giant over weight man who was so large he would take up two seats came walking down the aisle. He came up to me and said that seat beside me was for him.

I could not believe it, I was going to be squashed the whole way home! I am tall and I like to lift weights, so I also have very broad shoulders. I had half of my body in the aisle area. He also smelt like he was not wearing any deodorant so I was uncomfortable to say the least. Apart from all of this, I decided to just praise God and be joyful and witness to this man.

As soon as take off was finished I had the flight attendant tap me on my shoulder and ask me if I would like an upgrade. She told me there were two vacant seats up the front of the plane with my name on them. Wow! The plane was so full yet God saved two seats just for me. Wow, I Praised God again and said to God "You really look after me."

CHAPTER 13

PRAISE WALK

ೋ ೋ

I have included a `Praise Walk' exercise by Don Gossett for you.

A Challenge for a Seven Day Praise Walk.

DAY ONE: On this first day of your Praise Walk, endeavour to walk through each room of your home praising the Lord with each step. Your Praise Walk objective is to literally saturate and impregnate your life with God's presence (Psalm 22:3). As you pace and praise, the Holy One shall respond and reside in your praises - richly manifesting His presence. (See 2 Chronicles 5:13–14).

DAY TWO: Practice the beautiful art of lifting up your hands in praise as you stroll through your home (Psalm 63:3 – 4). The act of lifting up hands to the Lord is a demonstration of surrender to His Lordship. Reach out to Him in loving worship.

DAY THREE: Sing jubilant praises to God. You are commanded to "come before His presence with singing". (Psalm 100:2). Devote this wonderful day of your Praise Walk to "making melodies to the King" (Ephesians 5:19). It is not the quality of your voice that is important - even a 'joyful noise' pleases God! Raise your voice in triumph and glory to God. Magnify the Music-Maker who has put His song of praise in your mouth (Psalm 40:3). He loves to hear you sing to Him - savouring each note and melody.

DAY FOUR: Fulfill God's expectations of you by continually sacrificing praise to Him. Subdue your senses and discipline your feelings to obey His command "to offer up the sacrifice of praise to God continually" (Hebrews 13:15). Be consistent and bless Him when you feel like it - and even when you don't!

DAY FIVE: Focus on honouring the Lord for His goodness to you. Enumerate His wonderful works in your life (Psalm 103:1 – 5). Forget not His benefits: bless the Lord with all that is within you for His salvation, healing, protection, spiritual and material blessings. Permeate each room of your home with phrases of praise and thanksgiving.

DAY SIX: Rejoice as you move through your home. Exalt the Lord of Heaven who is your source of joy (Psalm 63:5). While walking, praise Jesus adoringly with a variety of names and titles to describe His character and nature.

DAY SEVEN: Long ago the children of Israel were commanded to march around the walls of Jericho for seven days (Joshua 6). On the seventh day, they were instructed to shout praises to the Lord. When they shouted praises, the walls fell down. On this seventh day of your Praise Walk, shout praises to God... believing the walls, obstacles and oppressions that beset your life will fall down!

Now, stand right up and make these good confessions aloud:

1. I possess continual guidance, for I confess,
"The Lord shall guide thee continually"
Isaiah 58:11.

2. I possess eternal life, for I confess,
"My sheep hear My voice... and I give unto them eternal life."
John 10:27-28.

3. I possess the peace of God, for I confess,
"The peace of God which passeth all understanding,
shall keep your hearts and minds through Christ Jesus our Lord"
Philippians 4:7.

4. I possess freedom from fear, for I confess,
"I the Lord thy God will hold thy right hand, saying unto thee, fear not"   Isaiah 41:13.

5. I possess bountiful blessings financially, for I confess,
"He which soweth bountifully shall reap also bountifully"
2 Corinthians 9:6.

5. I possess supernatural help in every situation, for I confess,
"My help cometh from the Lord, which made heaven and earth."
Psalm 121:2.

6. I possess good, for I confess,
"Acquaint now thyself with Him, and be at peace:
Thereby good shall come unto thee"
Job 22:21.

7. I possess peace with my enemies, for I confess,
"When a man's ways please the Lord, He maketh even his enemies to be at peace with him"
Proverbs 16:7.

8. I possess the ability to be a positive blessing, for I confess,
"So will I save you, and Ye shall be a blessing"
Zechariah 8:13.

9. I possess wholesome, sound sleep at night, for I confess,
"He giveth His beloved sleep"
Psalm 127:2.

10. I possess the assurance my labour in the Lord is fruitful, for I confess, "For as much as ye know that your labour is not in vain in the Lord"
1 Corinthians 15:58.

11. I possess as a faith man, abounding blessings, for I confess,
"A faithful man shall abound with blessings"
Proverbs 28:20.

12. I possess strength for my day, for I confess,
"As thy days, so shall thy strength be"
Deuteronomy 33:25.

13. I possess special honour from my Father, for I confess,
"If any man serve Me, him will my Father honour"
John 12:26.

Praise Report 6

Kingdom Finance Through Praise

A number of years ago now, we had a visiting minister from Alabama, named Scott Webb, come and minister at our church. Pastor Scott spoke on financial increase through speaking the word and praise. He shared about how the Lord had laid it on his heart to sow a sum of money into another ministry. He was then to believe God for his harvest. Pastor Scott then went on to say how for three years he, 'Praised God' that someone would sow into his ministry $300,000 US dollars in one lump sum. I'll never forget that day when Pastor Scott shared how for three years he would confess, "Praise God, someone gives me $300,000 in one lump sum for the work of the ministry." He said he didn't say it every day, but just whenever he would think of it. Sometimes he would repeat it over and over,-"Praise God, someone gives me $300,000 in one lump for the work of this ministry."

He kept up the praise and the confession of his faith without wavering. He told us that regularly, (but not everyday,) he would stop what he was doing and just 'Praise the Lord' for his goodness and that someone would give him $300,000 for the work of the ministry. He remembers the day when, after 3 years, someone walked into his office and handed him a $300,000 cheque for the work of the ministry! He now confesses for $1,000,000 in a (one lump sum) cheque for the work of the ministry!!

Well, you can imagine my joy, as a Pastor, hearing this testimony about how this money manifested through faith and praise! So from that day, Kerrie and I started to confess, "Praise God someone gives us a $100,000 cheque, in one lump sum or an asset to sell for the work of the ministry. We started at $100,000 because we felt it was a comfortable faith goal for us. Up until that point in time, the largest single donation our ministry had ever received was $25,000 Australian dollars.

We have and always will be big sowers into missions. World Harvest Ministries feeds over 300 children a week in India through it's orphanage, schools and education programs. Together we look after widows, feed the hungry and clothe the naked in places around the world where poverty has caused great stress and grief. To the best of our ability, we respond to natural disasters as we partner with ministries working in the affected areas in practical ways.

Well, 'Praise God!' One day (after about eight years of confessing, "In the name of Jesus, Father we thank you that someone gives us a cheque for $100,000 for the work of the ministry."), a faithful man handed me a cheque for $100,000 for the work of the ministry! Hallelujah! With this finance, we were able to make a huge difference in the lives of many poor people. We were able to finish some building work, purchase a missions transport car in India (our ministry in India desperately needed a four wheel drive to access remote, poor areas), a motor bike for a Baptist pastor in India, another motor bike for a relief worker, and many other feeding and medical projects and, most importantly, reach many people with the love and Gospel of our Lord Jesus Christ. Wow! What we were able to accomplish with that seed gift was truly amazing!

We now confess, "Praise God, someone gives us in one lump sum, or an asset to sell, $300,000 for the work of the ministry." We keep stretching our faith by also confessing "Praise God someone gives us in one lump sum, $1,000,000 for the work of the ministry." The bible says we go from 'Faith to Faith' and from 'Glory to Glory'. God has many precious and exceedingly great promises for you, the believer, in His Kingdom. He has told us in His Word that He has given us the 'keys' of the Kingdom! Praise is one of those powerful keys that unlock Kingdom blessing, Kingdom authority and Kingdom provision for your life.

Chapter 14

One Hundred Praise Scriptures

೪ ಳಿ

1-2. 2 Chronicles 5:13-14
"It came even to pass,
as the trumpeters and singers were as one,
to make one sound to be heard in praising and
thanking the Lord,
and when they lifted up their voice with the trumpets and
cymbals and instruments of music, and praised the Lord,
saying,
'For He is good; for His mercy endureth for ever: that then
the house was filled with a cloud, even the house of the Lord'
so that the priests could not stand to minister
by reason of the cloud:
for the glory of the Lord had filled the house of God."

3-4. 2 Chronicles 20:21-22
"And when he had consulted with the people,
he appointed singers unto the Lord,
and that should praise the beauty of holiness,
as they went out before the army, and to say,
Praise the Lord; for His mercy endureth for ever."

5.   Psalm 5:11
"But let all those that put their trust in Thee rejoice: let them ever shout for joy, because Thou defendest them: let them also that love Thy name be joyful in Thee."

6.   Psalm 7:17
"I will praise the Lord according to His righteousness and will sing praise to the name of the Lord most high."

7-8.   Psalm 9:1-2
"I will praise Thee O Lord, with my whole heart;
I will shew forth all Thy marvelous works.
I will be glad and rejoice in Thee:
I will sing praise to Thy Name.
O Thou Most High."

9.   Psalm 9:11
"Sing praises to the Lord, which dwelleth in Zion: declare among the people His doings."

10.   Psalm 13:6
"I will sing unto the Lord,
because He hath dealt bountifully with me."

11.   Psalm 18:3
"I will call upon the Lord,
Who is worthy to be praised:
so shall I be saved from mine enemies."

12.   Psalm 18:49
"Therefore will I give thanks unto Thee, O Lord, among the heathen and sing praises unto Thy name."

13. Psalm 22:3
"But Thou art holy,
O Thou that inhabits the praises of Israel."

14. Psalm 28:6
"Blessed be the Lord,
because He hath heard the voice of my supplications."

15. Psalm 29:2
"Give unto the Lord the glory due unto His name:
worship the Lord in the beauty of holiness."

16. Psalm 32:11
"Be glad in the Lord, and rejoice, ye righteous:
and shout for Joy, all ye that are upright in heart."

17. Psalm 33:1
"Rejoice in the Lord O ye righteous:
for praise is comely for the upright."

18. Psalm 34:1
"I will bless the Lord at all times:
His praise shall continually be in my mouth."

19. Psalm 35:18
"I will give Thee thanks in the great congregation:
I will praise Thee among much people."

20. Psalm 35:27
"Let them shout for joy, and be glad,
that favour my righteous cause:
yea, let them say continually, let the Lord be magnified,
which hath pleasure in the prosperity of his servant."

21. Psalm 40:3
"And He hath put a new song in my mouth,
even praise unto our God:
many shall see it, and fear,
and shall trust in the Lord."

22. Psalm 42:11
"Why art thou cast down, O my soul?
And why art thou disquieted within me?
Hope thou in God: for I shall yet praise Him
who is the health of my countenance, and my God."

23. Psalm 43:5
"Why art thou cast down, O my soul?
And why art thou disquieted within me?
Hope in God, for I shall yet praise Him,
who is the health of my countenance, and my God."

24. Psalm 47:1
"O clap your hands, all ye people;
shout unto God with the voice of triumph."

25. Psalm 47:6
"Sing praises to God, sing praises:
sing praises unto our King, sing praises."

26. Psalm 48:1
"Great is the Lord,
and greatly to be praised in the city of our God,
in the mountain of His holiness."

27. Psalm 50:23
"Whoso offereth praise glorifieth Me,
and to him that ordereth his conversation aright will
I shew the salvation of God."

28. Psalm 51:15
"O Lord, open Thou my lips;
and my mouth shall shew forth Thy praise."

29. Psalm 52:9
"I will praise Thee for ever,
because Thou hast done it:
and I will wait on Thy name;
for it is good before Thy saints."

30. Psalm 54:6
"I will freely sacrifice unto Thee:
I will praise Thy name, O Lord; for it is good."

31. Psalm 56:4
"In God I will praise His Word,
in God I have put my trust;
I will not fear what flesh can do unto me."

32. Psalm 56:10
"In God will I praise His word:
in the Lord will I praise His Word."

33. Psalm 56:12
"Thy vows are upon me, O God:
I will render praises unto Thee."

34.   Psalm 57:7
      "My heart is fixed, O God, my heart is fixed:
        I will sing and give praise."

35.   Psalm 57:9
        "I will praise Thee,
        O Lord, among the people:
        I will sing unto Thee among the nations."

36-38. Psalm 63:3-5
        "Because Thy loving-kindness is better than life,
          my lips shall praise Thee.
        Thus will I bless Thee while I live,
          I will lift up Thy name.
        My soul shall be satisfied as with marrow and fatness,
          and my mouth shall praise Thee with joyful lips."

39.   Psalm 66:2
        "Sing forth the honour of His name,
          make His praise glorious."

40.   Psalm 66:8
        "O bless our God, ye people,
        and make the voice of His praise to be heard."

41.   Psalm 67:3
        "Let the people praise Thee, O God;
          let all the people praise Thee."

42.   Psalm 67:5
        "Let the people praise Thee, O God;
          let all the people praise Thee."

43. Psalm 68:19
"Blessed be the Lord who daily loadeth us with benefits, even the God of our salvation."

44. Psalm 69:30
"I will praise the name of God with a song, and will magnify Him with thanksgiving."

45. Psalm 71:14
"But I will hope continually, and will yet praise Thee more and more."

46. Psalm 92:1
"It is a good thing to give thanks unto the Lord, and to sing praises unto Thy name, O Most High."

47-48. Psalm 95:1-2
"O come, let us sing unto the Lord: let us make a joyful noise to the rock of our salvation. Let us come before His presence with thanksgiving, and make a joyful noise unto Him with psalms."

49-52 Psalm 100:1-4
"Make a joyful noise unto the Lord, all ye lands. Serve the Lord with gladness: come before His presence with singing. Know ye that the Lord, He is God: it is He that hath made us, and not we ourselves; we are His people, and the sheep of His pasture. Enter into His gates with thanksgiving, and into His courts with praise: be thankful unto Him, and bless His name."

53-54. Psalm 103:1-2
> "Bless the Lord, O my soul:
> and all that is within me, bless His holy name.
> Bless the Lord, O my soul,
> and forget not all His benefits."

55-56. Psalm 105:1-2
> "O give thanks unto the Lord; call upon His name:
> make known His deeds among the people.
> Sing unto Him, sing psalms unto Him;
> talk ye of all His wondrous works."

57. Psalm 106:2
> "Who can utter the mighty acts of the Lord?
> Who can shew forth all His praise?"

58. Psalm 106:12
> "Then believed they His words;
> they sang His praise."

59. Psalm 107:8
> "Oh that men would praise the Lord for His goodness
> and for His wonderful works to the children of men."

60. Psalm 107:15
> "Oh that men would praise the Lord for His goodness
> and for His wonderful works to the children of men."

61. Psalm 107:21
> "Oh that men would praise the Lord for His goodness
> and for His wonderful works to the children of men."

62. Psalm 107:31
"Oh that men would praise the Lord for His goodness and for His wonderful works to the children of men."

63. Psalm 113:3
"From the rising of the sun unto the going down of the same the Lord's name is to be praised."

64. Psalm 134:2
"Lift up your hands in the sanctuary and bless the Lord."

65-67. Psalm 145:1-3
"I will extol Thee, my God, O King; and I will bless Thy name for ever and ever. Everyday will I bless Thee; and I will praise Thy name for ever and ever. Great is the Lord, and greatly to be praised."

68. Psalm 147:1
"Praise ye the Lord: for it is good to sing praises unto our God; for it is pleasant; and praise is beautiful."

69. Psalm 150:6
"Let every thing that hath breath praise the Lord. Praise ye the Lord."

70-71. Luke 17:15-16
"And one of them, when he saw that he was healed, turned back and with a loud voice glorified God, and fell down on his face at His feet, giving Him thanks: and he was a Samaritan."

72. Luke 18:43
> "And immediately he received his sight,
> and followed Him, glorifying God:
> and all the people, when they saw it,
> gave praise unto God."

73-74. Luke 19:37-38
> "And when He was come nigh,
> even now at the descent of the mount of Olives,
> the whole multitude of the disciples began to
> rejoice and praise God with a loud voice
> for all the mighty works that they had seen;
> saying, Blessed be the King
> that cometh in the name of the Lord:
> peace in heaven and glory in the highest."

75. Luke 24:53
> "And they were continually in the temple,
> praising and blessing God."

76. Acts 2:47
> "Praising God,
> and having favour with all the people.
> And the Lord added to the church daily
> such as should be saved."

77. Acts 3:8
> "And he leaping up stood, and walked,
> and entered with them into temple,
> walking and leaping,
> and praising God."

78. Acts 16:25
"And at midnight Paul and Silas prayed,
and sang praises unto God:
And the prisoners heard them."

79. 1 Corinthians 14:16
"Else, when Thou shalt bless with the spirit,
how shall he that occupieth the room of the unlearned
say Amen at Thy giving of thanks,
seeing he understandeth not what Thou sayest."

80. 2 Corinthians 9:15
"Thanks be unto God for His unspeakable gift."

81. Ephesians 5:4
"Neither filthiness, nor foolish talking,
nor jesting, which are not convenient;
but rather giving of thanks."

82-83. Ephesians 5:19-20
"Speaking to yourselves
in psalms and hymns and spiritual songs,
singing and making melody in your heart to the Lord;
giving thanks always for all things
unto God and the Father
in the name of our Lord Jesus Christ."

84. Philippians 4:4
"Rejoice in the Lord always: and again I say rejoice."

85. Philippians 4:6
"Be careful for nothing;
but in every thing by prayer
and supplication with thanksgiving
let your requests be made known unto God."

86. Colossians 1:12
"Giving thanks unto the Father,
which hath made us fit to be partakers of the
inheritance of the saints in light."

87. Colossians 2:7
"Rooted and built up in Him,
and stablished in the faith,
as ye have been taught,
abounding therein with thanksgiving."

88. Colossians 3:15
"And let the peace of God rule in your hearts,
to which also you are called in one body,
and be ye thankful."

89. Colossians 4:2
"Continue in prayer,
and watch in the same with thanksgiving."

90. 1 Thessalonians 5:18
"In every thing give thanks:
for this is the will of God in
Christ Jesus concerning you."

91. 1 Timothy 4:4
"For every creature of God is good,
and nothing to be refused,
if it be received with thanksgiving."

92. 2 Timothy 3:1
"In the last days, perilous times shall come,
for men shall become... unthankful."

93. Hebrews 13:15
"By Him therefore let us offer
the sacrifice of praise to God continually,
that is, the fruit of our lips,
giving thanks to His name."

94. 1 Peter 2:9
"But ye are a chose generation,
a royal priesthood,
a holy nation, a peculiar people;
that ye should shew forth the praises of Him
who hath called you out of darkness
into His marvelous light."

95-100. Revelation 19:1, 3-7
"And after these things I heard a great voice
of much people in heaven, saying, Alleluia;

Salvation, and glory, and honour, and power,
unto the Lord our God:
And again they said, Alleluia:
And her smoke rose up for ever and ever.

And the four and twenty elders and the four beasts fell down
and worshipped God that sat on the throne,
saying, Amen; Alleluia.
And a voice came out of the throne, saying,
Praise our God, all ye His servants,
and ye that fear him,
both small and great.
And I heard as it were the voice of a great multitude
and as the voice of many waters,
and as the voice of mighty thunderings,
saying Alleluia;
for the Lord God omnipotent reigneth.
Let us be glad and rejoice,
and give honour to Him:
for the marriage of the Lamb is come
and his wife hath made herself ready."

I encourage you to memorise these praise Scriptures, as they will become the power of God released in your confession. The Holy Spirit will then be able to quicken these verses to you, time and time again, to reassure your heart of God's victory in your life and circumstances.

REMEMBER:

JESUS CHRIST, THE SAME YESTERDAY, TODAY, AND FOREVER - HEBREWS 13:8.

You are very special. GOD LOVES YOU. He sent His son Jesus Christ who died for you and was raised from the dead. You are a somebody, because you were created by God and He doesn't make nobodies. You are God's best, His dream, His idea.

Jeremiah 29: 11-14(a) NKJV
"For I know the plans I have for you," declares the Lord, "plans to prosper you and not to harm you, plans to give you hope and a future. Then you will call upon Me and come and pray to Me, and I will listen to you. You will seek Me and find Me when you seek Me with all your heart. I will be found by you, declares the Lord…"

If you are reading this book for the first time and you are not sure that Jesus is the Lord of your life, you need to pray the prayer below and invite Jesus to be your personal Lord and Saviour. When you pray this prayer, please write to us and let us know of this important decision that you have made. We will gladly send you some free information on what it means to be born again and have Christ as the Lord of your life.

WHAT TO PRAY TO BE SAVED

HEAVENLY FATHER,
I BELIEVE THAT JESUS CHRIST IS THE SON OF GOD,
WHO HAS COME IN THE FLESH.
I THANK YOU THAT YOU SENT YOUR SON, JESUS,
TO DIE ON THE CROSS FOR ME.

I REPENT OF ALL MY SINS,
AND ASK FOR YOUR FORGIVENESS.

JESUS, PLEASE COME INTO MY HEART RIGHT NOW
BY YOUR SPIRIT, BE MY PERSONAL LORD AND
SAVIOUR.
I BELIEVE WITH MY HEART AND I CONFESS WITH MY
MOUTH THAT JESUS CHRIST IS LORD.
FATHER, BAPTISE ME WITH YOUR HOLY SPIRIT
AND CHANGE ME INTO THE KIND OF PERSON
YOU WANT ME TO BE.

I AM NOW A CHILD OF THE ALMIGHTY GOD.
THANK YOU FOR SAVING ME.
IN JESUS' NAME,
AMEN.

DON'T FORGET

If you have just prayed this prayer for the first time,
or if we can be of any assistance,
or for a free booklet and further information
on what it means to be born again, or to get a full list of books
and teachings, I have prepared to enable you to win in life
through Jesus Christ,
please contact:

World Harvest Ministries
PO Box 90 BALD HILLS QLD 4036
AUSTRALIA
Phone: +61 7 3261 4555.
Email: general@whm.org.au
Web: www.whm.org.au
www.shaunmarler.com
Facebook: www.facebook.com/worldharvestmin

Please write in and share with us your testimonies
of how this teaching on
PRAISE POWER
has made a difference in your life
and brought you into what God has for you.
May this force be with you, as you continually praise Him.

"Your best is yet to come!"

Love in Jesus,

Dr Shaun Marler.

FAITH WORK

GOD HAS WONDERFUL THINGS IN STORE FOR

Fill your name in here: _____

Speak the above confession ten times -
BECAUSE PRAISE IS VOCAL.

MEMORY VERSES.

1 John 4:4
"Little children, you are of God
and have defeated and overcome them,
because He Who lives in you
is greater than he who is in the world."

Romans 8:31
"What shall we then say to these things?
If God be for us, who can be against us?"

John 1:12
But as many as received Him,
to them gave He power to become the sons of God,
even to them that believed on His name:

Psalm 34:3
"O magnify the Lord with me,
and let us exalt His name together."

Proverbs 12:25 (NKJV)
Anxiety in the heart of man causes depression,
But a good word makes it glad.

ABOUT THE AUTHOR

Dr. Shaun Marler is the Senior Pastor and co-founder with his wife Kerrie of World Harvest Ministries, an international organisation based in Queensland, Australia, World Harvest Ministries is committed to carrying out the Great Commission of Jesus our Lord, in feeding the hungry, clothing the naked, visiting the widows and orphans in their affliction, and preaching the Good News to the poor.

World Harvest Ministries currently has programs in India where the poor and destitute are given free medical treatment, orphan homes where children are fed, accommodated and educated, a ministry to widows who have been abandoned by society and a program to feed people with leprosy.

A portion of the proceeds of the sale of this book goes towards this valuable work. Which is making a huge difference in the lives of others!